When Hell Trembles

When Hell Trembles

and Other Sermons for Revival

James P. Wesberry

BAKER BOOK HOUSE
Grand Rapids, Michigan

ISBN: 0-8010-9558-1

Printed in the United States of America

To

the members of

Morningside Baptist Church of Atlanta

and to

thousands of friends I love

and will love forever

Contents

Foreword

Someone recently wrote that James P. Wesberry is "the only man I know who has become a living legend." Dr. Wesberry, my beloved pastor and intimate friend, is just that.

Dr. Wesberry's motivation is his love for individuals, and he can communicate that love. That people respond to his love is apparent from his long tenure as pastor of Atlanta's Morningside Baptist, one of America's great churches.

Dr. Wesberry is a man "crying in the wilderness" with the answer to man's deepest yearnings. The sermons in this book waste no words in clearly reflecting the author's thinking. His theology is sound and his love compelling. These sermons will motivate readers to become part of the revival that our country needs.

W. D. Lawes
Associate Director, Field Service
Division of Evangelism
Home Mission Board
Southern Baptist Convention

Preface

Revival.

What does it mean?

According to Webster, *revive* means recover from a state of neglect, raise from languor or depression, rejuvenate or renew. Each definition gives us a unique slant on the meaning of the word for our times.

An underground spring is washing the church clean today. From the grass roots up, the church is *reviving*. It is "recovering from a state of neglect," a state into which it fell during the last two decades when man acquiesced in materialism and other shoddy values.

Are we among those cleansing the church, recovering it from neglect? Or in the face of the new Christian march do we draw the shawl of complacency about us, shrug our shoulders, and sigh, "But what can *I* do?"

If we care about the cause of Christ in the world—beginning with our own families and neighborhoods—we will work for revival in another sense. We will revive ourselves—"raise ourselves from the languor and depression" that drive us into isolation and prevent our reaching out to others.

God has made it possible for us to reach out. He sent His Son to make it clear that He accepts us as we are. That acceptance is sufficient to batter down the doors of isolation and to open our hearts to others. When we become "new creatures" in Christ, we are rejuvenated, renewed, revived in the Spirit. As believers, we are free to accept ourselves, and each other, as Christ has accepted us.

If we are interested in our own renewal, actively committed to caring for our brothers and dependent on God for direction, we will be able to carry forward the revival of the church.

These chapters are offered in the hope that they will help us discover the direction of revival—recovery, renewal, rejuvenation—for our lives and for the church.

Yes, because God cared, we can care and can begin to revive the world where we are!

When Hell Trembles /1

Matthew 18:20

For where two or three are gathered together in my name, there am I in the midst of them.

In C. S. Lewis' *Screwtape Letters,* one of Satan's agents on earth, whose assignment is to keep a man from becoming a Christian, is worried because his intended victim has joined the church. But Screwtape assures him that "there is no need to despair as long as the victim does not see the Church itself as we see her, spread out through all time and space and rooted in eternity, terrible as an army of banners. That, I confess, is a spectacle which makes our boldest tempters uneasy." This passage expresses a great truth: the Christian banner strikes fear into the very heart of hell.

What Is Hell?

What is hell? Let us look at it from five directions:

1. Hell on earth is the *state of sin* into which we are born. Sir Thomas Browne wrote, "I feel sometimes a hell within myself." This feeling is grounded in the fact that "before sin is an act, it is a state," as Paul Tillich said. God accepts us in our sinful condition.

2. Hell is *separation from each other.* We live crowded together, but we are alone. Even our most intimate relationships are less than intimate. This is especially true during crises.

3. Hell is *separation from God,* a prison in time and space from which the soul never breaks free from the immediate and temporal.

4. Hell is a *lack of destination.*

5. Hell is the final *abode of the impenitent,* those who reject Jesus Christ. The Bible makes this quite clear.

Can anything make hell tremble? If God be for us, may we expect Him to give us an instrument of divine power which will enable us to stand and move against the kingdoms of this world? What is that instrument?

It is the church of Jesus Christ, which wars against the evils of the world, against Satan, against principalities and powers. The "body of Christ"—the church—is not a mystical, static notion, but a dynamic, living creation, completely committed to heaven in its struggle with hell. In the form of the church God thrusts Himself into the world in a mighty onslaught against the kingdoms of evil. Under its banners we can go forward.

The church can make hell tremble!

The Church Is the Answer

God knew that He could not destroy evil unless He came Himself into the world where sin reigns; He had to beat it on its own territory. It was costly to enter enemy territory, but He did it for our sakes. He paid the price; He is still paying it; and He will be paying it for a long time to come. Was it worthwhile?

Think of our American soldiers in the Pacific and the monuments to their heroism. Think of the cross, the symbol of Christ's victory and sacrifice for us, and of the glorious resurrection, when Jesus defeated our last great enemy.

The day God invaded this earth was our V-Day. The church is the living power of the resurrection. The power that conquered sin and death, the power of the risen Christ, is alive at the heart of the church.

The enemy still exists; he occupies plenty of territory where we live. But, if this resurrection power is active in the church, then hell has reason to tremble. For here is a force adequate to hold back the tide of evil and dethrone the devil. Ours is a power purchased at a supreme price. No wonder Jesus said to Peter; "And the gates of hell shall not prevail against the church."

It is a marvelous feeling to follow in the footsteps of the early Christians who found a new life in the power of the resurrection.

We walk where they walked. We bow where they bowed and rose to go out, victorious over temper, hatred, weakness, and fear because God held them in the hollow of His hand.

We may find power outside the church, but it is usually an overflow from the church; and, unless it leads back into the church, it usually shrivels and dies. The saddest thing of all is that sometimes this power dies within the church itself.

The music of the church should never be the same as the music of the world. The same power that nerved the church through her turbulent history—the persecutions in Rome, costly missionary advances, and campaigns against evil and idolatry—will see her through the present and the future. Hell is afraid of such a church.

Dr. Robert E. Luccock has written in his book, *If God be for us:* "Hell begins on the day when God grants us a clear vision of all that we might have achieved, of all the gifts which we have wasted, of all that we might have done that we did not do. For me the conception of hell lies in two words: 'too late'."

Peter and Judas both looked into hell, but Peter was resurrected. At the heart of the church is God's forgiveness. Those who receive it can be rocks; they go through hell and come out with great power. No wonder hell trembles at the sight of the church whose banners fly high for the risen Christ.

T. S. Eliot in "The Cocktail Party" says, "Hell is oneself; hell is alone, the other figures in it merely projections. There is nothing to escape from—or to. One is always alone."

One person alone is no match for the powerful entrenched armies of evil, the powers of darkness. Even great masses of isolated individuals are no match for the kingdoms of hell on the march. The world will not hear the message of a divided church. The world must see a bond of fellowship between those who confess primary allegiance to God through Jesus Christ.

Do we want to see hell tremble? Where two or three are gathered together in Christ's love, there will He be, and this kind of communion shakes hell.

The group of nine that climbed the 26,000-foot peak of Annapurna shared the joy and pain of toil, and faced death as none of them could have faced it alone. The leader of the 1950 expedition,

Maurice Herzog, reflected: "My fervent wish is that the nine of us who were united in the face of death should remain fraternally united through life." They were as one man. In their discovery of community in the face of death, they discovered the greatest secret of life—communion in which all are fused together by the spirit of a great pursuit.

The church is a whole community of people disciplined by a single loyalty and love, and united in the face of death. At the end of his book, Herzog wrote, "There are other Annapurnas in the lives of men"—great summits to ascend, not in the Himalayas but towering above the lowlands where we live. When we join a Christian fellowship, we join a company which binds us to its heart, a company of those who walk together now and who have walked before. We no longer climb alone.

This is true of any church. Some whom you know have broken the trail. Others are climbing with you; they may not know all your hardships, but they will help you on the rope when the going is steep. Others in the camp are far down the slopes you have already climbed, and your love surrounds them as they climb. What a blessing to climb in such company!

A man stood on the church steps watching a congregation assemble for worship. He knew most of the people well. As he watched them, he thought to himself that they were a pretty sorry bunch: weak men and women, spineless in character, full of deceit. If the whole were merely the sum of its parts, it would be a sad assembly indeed!

Then he went into the church and joined the company in communion. Suddenly he felt an invisible "plus" element added to the sum of the whole. He discovered that, in Christ, the whole is greater than the sum of its parts. As the congregation stood to sing "My Faith Looks Up to Thee," he was sure that something more than a company of frail men and women was in that room. True communion has a lifting and delivering power which hell cannot bind.

Hell is a prison of time and place, keeping all eyes on the clock and the ground. The devil's strategy is to focus man's attention on petty annoyances, to allure him into feverish activity, to busy him with "being busy."

This leaves no time for a man to lift his eyes to the hills and discover whence cometh his help. He feels no need to touch the hem of God's garments, has no desire to storm the gates of heaven. The devil wants men to think of this prison as their homeland. Then life will wither away or wear itself out with no transfusion from beyond, no blessing from above. Life will go out like a candle. This is hell.

But, let a man see the church banners flying, enter, worship, and fling his soul upward to the heights, and hell is wise enough to know that it should tremble.

For men at worship might discover their true homeland. They might discover that life is more than ailments and annoyances, clocks and calendars, looking glasses and yardsticks. One of the great purposes of the church is to point and lift the soul toward God and away from anxiety and fussiness, to secure release from the prison of time and space.

Heaven Makes Hell Tremble

A man who sees nothing beyond the grave is living in hell already. The devil doesn't fear the church as long as it focuses on this life. The bigger the church, the busier, the more efficient, the better the devil likes it. In this matter he is smarter than the average church member!

We hear many say, "Let's not worry about heaven; we don't have time for 'pie in the sky' religion. Let's make this the best of all possible worlds." This sounds modern, enlightened, emancipated. But it makes the devil laugh; he knows better. He knows that a church concerned with its eternal destiny and convinced that all the souls in it possess eternal life threatens a loose world. For even death is swallowed up for those who regard their lives as expendable for righteousness' sake. They shine like stars in the world; no darkness can extinguish them. Joseph Fort Newton said, "No promise is given to a . . . beleaguered church that apologizes for its gospel. Only to a church militant against evil, storming the final fortress of wrong—for no other is a church —shall be given the keys of the kingdom."

The tremendous conviction of eternal destiny is found only in a resurrection society where the church storms the very center of hell itself.

The church at her best suffers condemnation; she is more aware of her deepest sins than are her critics. But somewhere at her heart is One who promises that, wherever two or three are gathered, He will be there. Whatever her flaws, the church is still a kingdom of love, an island in a sea of evil, because at her center is the Lord Jesus Christ; and she is joined by invisible bonds to a far greater kingdom beyond the horizon.

A church being revived, awakened, coming to itself; a church rededicated, praying, giving, singing, visiting; a church on the march in an advanced program; a church with all its banners flying; a church soul-winning, attending, witnessing, united —this is what strikes terror in hell.

The enemies of the church can climb to the moon and draw a curtain over her silvery face, or to the sun and with their feeble breath blow out its glowing flames, easier than they can put out the light of Jesus Christ, the Sun of righteousness, or darken the glory of His church, which is as "fair as the moon, clear as the sun, and terrible as an army with banners."

Life's Biggest Business / 2

Matthew 5:43-48

Be ye therefore perfect, even as your Father which is in heaven is perfect (v. 48).

What is the biggest business in the world?

Opinions differ. President Eisenhower referred to the U.S. government as big business. Certainly that is true. Even state government is big business; the auditor's books alone tell us that!

What about farming? Think of the acreage devoted to raising crops. And how about cattle, oil, automobiles, space, banking, tobacco, and liquor?

A friend of mine has said that the biggest truth in the world is that Jesus saves. If this is so, then surely the business of being Christian is the biggest business in the world.

Do you agree? Some don't. Some who do not are ignorant of Christianity. They don't know what it means to be Christian. They do not know the history, heroism, achievements, power, and miracles of the Christian faith; they know only the mistakes, the failures, the travesties committed in the name of religion.

Others who do not see Christianity as the biggest business are Christians in name only, whose names are on church rolls and who know the historical facts, but who know none of the thrill of the Christian life. They are *in* the church, but not *of* it. Their church membership is less important than their membership in a civic club, a social organization, a fraternity, a sorority, or a political party. They love the ritual and substitute ceremony for personal sacrifice. Christianity itself is vague, fantastic, impractical, or utopian.

Others are Christians who are nervous. They sit on the edge of their seats, holding on with all their might while waiting to see what happens next. If Christianity came under attack, they would wait nervously for the outcome, watching it fall to the foe. Some are those too nervous to sit in a service for an hour or more, but can sit in the cold for several hours and enjoy a football game. In church they become nervous. Or bored.

Others water down Christianity until it loses its heroic, prophetic, gripping proportions. They substitute for high Christian living an easy, comfortable, and therefore feeble religion, one that doesn't interfere with the way they live. They want to please themselves, not God. In the words of the late Dick Sheppard: "Primarily Christianity is a way of living, an attempt at a certain kind of life, and not a philosophy. In the first instance it has nothing to do with intellectualism or theology, nor even with membership in a society. Theology will, and churchmanship may, follow; but they are attempts to explain experience and aids to those who have determined to accept the way of living and the standard of conduct which Christ demands."

The Business of Believing

What does this business of being Christian involve?

First, it involves believing and trusting in a God like Jesus, a Christlike God, a Godlike Christ.

Believing in a God like Jesus isn't easy. It never has been. That is why Jesus was crucified. He claimed to be like God—to *be* God. "I and the Father are one."

Believing in a Supreme Architect, a Supreme Intelligence, a Master Mind is much easier than believing in a heavenly Father like Jesus who knows, loves, and cares. Belief in such a Father requires courage, faith, and fortitude. That He would love us enough to unveil Himself in the life and ministry of Jesus, who in the end died for us the death of a murderer and thief, not reluctantly but willingly, is beyond our comprehension. Why would God allow Himself to be crucified? Even Jesus cried, "My God, my God, why?"

Philip said, "Lord, show us the Father and it sufficeth us." He was asking, What is God like? Is there an older or a newer question? What shall we think of God? Is there a more fundamental question, a more searching inquiry? Jesus answered it for all times: "Have I been so long time with you, and yet hast thou not known me, Philip? he that hath seen me hath seen the Father; and how sayest thou then, Shew us the Father?" (John 14:8, 9)

Dr. Leslie D. Weatherhead's analysis of the comfort derived from believing that God is like Christ is the best I have read:

> So when I see him nailed to a cross and yet looking into the face of God and calling God "Father," I find myself saying over and over again that there are things I cannot understand, there are things which seem to contradict the loving nature of God; but if Jesus says that God is a Father, and if Jesus can live his life in the Father's hands, and be certain, by faith, that all will work out well in the end, I can leave my life to him, and I can commit to his capable hands the lives of others, and get them, even in the hour of darkness, to hold on in the dark. . . . For the God who, on Easter morning, vindicated the faith of Jesus will vindicate those who . . . risk everything for the belief that he is what Jesus said he was, even though they find what Jesus found, that Gethsemane and Calvary lie between.

A father whose only son, an uncommonly brilliant youth and the apple of his eye, met an untimely death in a railway accident, was struck with horrible grief. After the first paroxysm of grief passed, he went directly to his pastor's home. Finding the door ajar, he entered without knocking, went to the library where the pastor was studying, seized him by the arm roughly, and shouted, "Tell me, sir, where was God when my son was killed?" After a tense moment of silence, the wise and understanding shepherd said, "My dear friend, God was just where He was when His own son died."

The pastor's belief in a Christlike God enabled him to mediate blessed assurance and comfort to an aching heart. The father, encouraged by his pastor's words, pulled himself together and found the strength to climb those altar stairs that ascend through the darkness to God.

The Business of Forgiving

Second, the biggest business in the world is the Christlike business of forgiving one's enemies.

Louis Untermeyer describes the spirit of the world in *Heinrich Heine: Paradox and Poet:* " 'My nature is the most peaceful in the world,' [Heine] wrote with deceptive mildness. 'All I ask is a simple cottage, a decent bed, good food, some flowers in front of my window, and a few trees beside my door. Then, if God wanted to make me completely happy, he would let me enjoy the spectacle of six or seven of my enemies dangling from those trees. I would forgive them all the wrongs they have done me—forgive them from the bottom of my heart, for we must forgive our enemies. But not until they are hanged!' "

This sounds humorous until we realize how common are the poet's sentiments. Most of us find it extremely difficult to forgive our enemies: those who have insulted us; those who have hurt us deeply; those who have done us great harm. But we can pray for them and for ourselves. To forgive on Sundays and hate during the week is not enough. To love only your own class, creed, race, family, or country is to trifle with Christ's teaching and to fail pitifully in this great business of being a Christian. The history of Christianity shows plainly the rancor, prejudice, and ill will which so sadly mar the Christian witness.

Jesus' ministry is a good example of unprejudiced living. He got along successfully with a group of twelve intimates which included a fiery revolutionary; an affectionate mystic; a volatile enthusiast; a slow-moving, devoted martyr; a cautious skeptical hero; a guileless noble pietist; a thrifty, hardheaded businessman; and one misguided genius who turned traitor. When the Master failed to keep the latter from his treason, He broke Judas' heart by forgiving him and all others in death on the cross.

Jesus said, "I must be about my Father's business." I would like for the world to know that I am about my Father's business, and that business is forgiveness. I would say with the poet:

So let me draw you to the great forgiveness—
Not as one who stoops to save you,
Not as one who stands aside with counsel.
Nay, as one who says, "I too was poisoned with
 the flowers that sting, but now arisen,
I am struggling up the path beside you;
Rise and let us face these heights together."

"For if ye forgive men their trespasses, your heavenly Father will also forgive you" (Matt. 6:14).

The Business of Living and Dying

Working in the biggest business in the world involves, thirdly, living and dying by the ideals of Jesus.

Many regard Jesus' way as impractical, visionary, utopian, unattainable. What did He stand for? What were His ideals? There is no mystery about it; the answer is clearly stamped on the pages of the New Testament.

In a world where only the rich, the powerful, and the learned were important, Jesus taught that the rest—the poor, the undone, the disinherited—also mattered. To the Good Shepherd the lost sheep was as important as the ninety-nine safe in the fold.

In a world where hate was rampant, Jesus stood for the gospel of good will. Amid war and injustice and iniquity, He stood for peace and justice and righteousness. His great heart of love went out to all people.

In a world of low moral standards, Jesus lived sinlessly. He was tempted but did not yield. He refused to run with the crowd.

This troubled world awaits humans with the ideals of Jesus Christ—men and women of extraordinary patience, courtesy, kindness, courage, tact, justice, magnanimity, and good will.

When Artur Rubinstein was a guest in New York City, he was asked by his host if he would like to attend a church. "Yes," he replied, "if you can take me to a preacher who will tempt me to do the impossible." What greater challenge is there than the challenge of Jesus Christ: "Be ye therefore perfect, even as your Father which is in heaven is perfect." Perfection may not be possible, but being a Christian *is* possible. And in being Christians we will be about our Father's business—the biggest business in the world.

The Christian's Supreme Task / 3

Luke 14:23

. . . Go out into the highways and hedges, and compel them to come in, that my house may be filled.

The parable of the great feast vividly illustrates the central imperative of the Christian gospel: "Go out into the highways and hedges, and compel them to come in." This text should be blazed upon the walls of every church. Christianity is a going, growing, glowing religion. Jesus never intended His followers to stop moving. The Christian's inescapable imperative is, Go!

These are not my words. They are not the words of great preachers throughout the ages, however binding and inspiring these men have made them. They are the words of the Master, the Captain of our salvation, the commander-in-chief of Christian forces. All authority in heaven and on earth is His. "Take heed what [how] ye hear."

Christ's message to the impenitent sinner is, Woe! "I heard an angel flying, . . . saying, . . . Woe, woe, woe, to the inhabiters of the earth."

His message to the penitent sinner is, Ho! "Ho, every one that thirsteth, come ye to the waters."

His message to the saved sinner is, Go! "Go out into the highways and hedges, and compel them to come in." Christ's all-consuming passion is that we "go . . . and preach the kingdom of God" (Luke 9:60).

"Go, and do thou likewise" (Luke 10:37).

"Go ye therefore, and teach" (Matt. 28:19).

"Arise, let us go hence" (John 14:31).

It is "Go, go, go." This is the Son of God's authoritative command to His disciples.

> Onward Christian soldiers,
> Marching as to war,
> With the cross of Jesus
> Going on before!
> Christ, the royal Master,
> Leads against the foe;
> Forward into battle,
> See His banner go!

Our Almost Unlimited Opportunity

Jesus commanded us to go into the streets and lanes, the highways and hedges, into all the world. And we are only skimming our opportunities.

"The harvest truly is plenteous, but the labourers are few" (Matt. 9:37). We need to see the magnitude and plight of the lost millions in our nation. We need a vision.

To be realistic, during the last decade, Sunday school enrollment and attendance have suffered heavy losses.

All of this means that one hundred million people are not systematically studying the Word of God. How long can such a nation last?

When a pastor of a church of one thousand members was asked how many of those he considered Christian, he replied, "If you mean by that, those who come fairly regularly to the church service, or who belong to any auxiliary of the church, or who contribute to the church regularly, or who partake of the Lord's Supper, then I would be compelled to say that less than forty-five percent of my membership is really Christian."

This may not alarm you, but it does me. These people, who constitute the majority, are lost, without God, without Christ, without the church. Moreover, they are without hope. And the days are passing.

Our Supreme Task

Jesus' greatest challenge was, "Compel them to come in." Compel, He said. Quickly. The time is short. The door will soon be closed, and they will be standing on the outside, unprepared, without oil. They will perish. Sad as it is, they will be lost.

Compel means to persuade strongly, to drive or urge by force, to secure by bonds, to coerce. Jesus commands us to compel them with love.

Personal evangelism is not the work of the minister alone, regardless of what many think. When did you last win someone to Christ? Does this question embarrass you? Suppose your deaconship depended on your winning at least one soul to Christ every three months? Suppose no one could teach a Sunday school class who did not win one soul every three months? How many pastors, college teachers, presidents, and professors meet this requirement? How long has it been since someone was led to Christ by you? How long will it be? Will God ask these questions in judgment?

You may say, "Lord, I am unworthy." Jesus said, "None is worthy except by the grace of God." We are to give in accordance with our gifts.

Or, you may feel you have nothing to give away, that you can't afford to share your faith because you haven't enough for yourself. But is religion something to be hoarded?

Do you consider it presumptuous to ask someone, "Have you met God?" Do you fear the answer that one man got: "No, but I have met a very impudent man!" We can sympathize with this man but, if we are Christians, should we fear anything? We have to fulfill an obligation to God.

Maybe you want to win souls but don't know how. You say, "Pastor, I want to bring people into the kingdom. Teach me how to do it." You can do four things.

1. *Be convinced that the lost are lost.*

Do you believe that you are lost without Christ? Do you believe that you are going to hell if you do not accept Him? Do you believe that you are without hope unless you repent? If you vigorously answer these questions in the affirmative, you should feel strongly about the salvation of others.

2. *Be concerned for the lost.*

I recall a little girl who had a terminal disease. She told the minister she wanted to die, and when he asked why, she replied, "If I die, you would conduct the funeral, wouldn't you?"

"Yes," the minister replied, a little nonplused.

"Then you would get a chance to preach to my daddy and tell him about Jesus, and I'd die *six* times if he could hear it."

Suppose we all felt this way. Think what we might do for the world!

Jesus cared. From the heights of His deity to the depths of His humanity, He cared. From the glory of heaven to the gory cross, He cared. See His wounds; see His tears. He cared.

Jesus placed great value upon the individual. Remember Nicodemus, the woman at the well, Zaccheus, Lazarus, and countless others. He died to save one as much as He died to save all. Archbishop Fulton J. Sheen at age seventy-two was asked what he thought should be the central concern of the Christian movement today, and he answered, "The preciousness of the individual to Jesus Christ."

3. *Consecrate yourself to soul-winning.*

The purpose of the church is to win souls to Christ. "As the Father hath sent me, even so send I you." Heaven rejoices over one sinner who repents, not over ninety-nine who have already repented. If a church is not winning souls, it is not a New Testament church.

We are prevented from trying to win others to Christ only by the sin of self-love. If you have nothing to give away, you do not enjoy complete possession.

First, let us take stock of ourselves: why it is that we do not do more? are we too busy with other duties? are we not dedicated enough to God's work? People will believe God is in heaven when they see God in our hearts. They will see God in us if we believe God is love. A resurrected life is the strongest argument for the resurrection of Jesus.

Then, let us represent, not misrepresent, Christ. We can represent Him only by letting Christ live at the center of our lives; we can do this only by developing our devotional lives, our Bible-reading, and our prayer lives. Nothing will substitute for these.

A young artist who had struggled for years to achieve greatness visited the Louvre in Paris for the first time. As he stood before the great painting of a celebrated master, tears filled his eyes, and he said gratefully, "I too am a painter."

If ever you become discouraged and are tempted to give up, look into the face of Jesus and feel the spirit of victory enter your heart; see His patience, wisdom, leadership, and ability to win men, and exclaim to yourself, "I, too, am a soul-winner!"

The Spirit of God will reinforce your efforts.

4. *Commence today.*

First, let us wake up. It is day! Day is passing and we will be asleep long enough. We must work while it is day.

Don't ask, "What would you have me to do, Lord?" and wait for the answer; go to work immediately. Hold an office in the church, teach, sing. The opportunities are numberless. Your duty is self-evident. The very name Christian implies that we are to be like Christ, magnetized to magnetize! We are to tell the story, transmit Christianity, purify society, erect the cross in view of every creature, rescue the perishing!

You do not have to *win* someone, but you do have to *try*. Pray for him. Make some kind of contact. Borrow a book. Lend a book. Do a favor. Ask a favor. But make your plans today.

"We are not responsible for conversion, but we are responsible for contact," said A. T. Pierson. We can compel no man to decide for Christ, but we can compel every man to decide, by bringing him the gospel message, either for or against Christ. God will take care of the harvest if we sow the seeds.

Cities don't just grow by themselves, their growth depends upon their inhabitants. So the growth of your church depends on you. The spirit of the church, the kind, the size, all depend on you. Your church needs you.

A prospective member of one of our churches recently said that she wanted to belong to a church where she knew that she wouldn't be missed when she wasn't there. What kind of a church would that be? Would you want to belong to it? The kind of church you have—and the size of Christ's kingdom—depends upon you!

This is where we have fallen down. We aren't winning the world to the Lord. We aren't working. Do you ever speak a word? Do you offer to visit? to telephone? to invite others? To do so is to obey Jesus' command, "Compel them to come in."

Do we need a revival? Yes! Are you praying for one? We will have one if we meet God's conditions. We need only go to work.

Part of our problem is satisfaction with the church the way it is. Are we meeting people's needs, or have we failed? We have gained much land for God, but much remains to be possessed.

Is the church too cold? There seems to be a great lack of warmth. I hope that we are not like Israel of old, who had multiplied her defenced cities and her palaces, but had forgotten God, in whom was her strength. Our strength is in God. It is "not by might, nor by power, but by my spirit, saith the Lord." The Holy Ghost must guide us. The church's strength is in Almighty God. The strength of the church is a perpetual Pentecost.

We hear cries of "lapsed masses." But the masses have not lapsed; the church, full of elder brothers who do not want the masses to come home, has lapsed. There is no sympathy for the sinner, the wayfaring man.

I call our church to *repentance!* When the members do their duty, looking in the highways and hedges, the streets and lanes, there is recovery—there is revival. Then we will see the baptism of the Holy Ghost; then, and only then, will people climb trees to see Jesus!

I challenge you to determine to "go!" that God's house may be filled. His house has room for all, and all are welcome; if any will not come, others will take their places. But souls can be won only one by one.

The Problem of Weight / 4

Daniel 5:27

TEKEL; Thou art weighed in the balances, and art found wanting.

The place is Babylon. The year is 538 B.C. The Medes and the Persians surround the city, and King Nabonidus, who had gone on a military expedition and left his son Belshazzar in control of the kingdom, finds himself shut out.

This is one of the most dramatic events in history. Belshazzar, proud to be the supreme commander, had given a blasphemous banquet—magnificent, idolatrous, profane. One thousand lords attended with their wives and concubines. You can imagine the decorations—the lights, the food, the music and gowns, the jewels, the abundance of wine mixed with whiskey. The king and his friends drink and drink, all toasting "Long live the king." They forget their dignity. The music gets wilder, the laughter louder, the talk more obscene.

Belshazzar loses all decorum and reverence. He tells his servants to bring in the golden and silver vessels which Nebuchadnezzar had taken from the Temple in Jerusalem. This is blasphemy! These vessels are for holy use. But he defies God, has the vessels filled with Babylonian wine, and honors heathen deities.

Suddenly a horrible silence falls over the banquet hall. The king's eyes fasten on the wall above the candlestick where an armless hand is writing mysterious letters. Terribly frightened, he suddenly sobers. "The king's countenance changed, and his thoughts troubled him, so that the joints of his loins were loosed, and his knees smote one against another."

Slowly he pulls himself together. He is perplexed; he cannot explain what he has seen. He calls his soothsayers, enchanters, astrologists, wise men. They know nothing. He calls Daniel and offers him fabulous gifts to interpret the handwriting on the wall. But Daniel rebukes the king, disdaining his proffered gifts. He tells Belshazzar that his blasphemy caused the writing to appear, and he interprets the writing:

Mene means, "God hath numbered thy kingdom, and finished it."

Tekel means, "Thou art weighed in the balances, and art found wanting."

Peres means, "Thy kingdom is divided, and given to the Medes and Persians.

"Mene, Mene, Tekel, Upharsin!"

Did the hilarity continue? No! The interpretation was true; the end was at hand; doom was imminent! Louder and louder were the sounds of the soldiers' feet. Darius and his army broke open the brass gates with a terrific pounding. Belshazzar and his lords tried to close the doors in terror, but the swords flashed, and "in that night was Belshazzar the king of the Chaldeans slain."

Belshazzar was weighed on God's scales and found wanting.

How God Measures

When you and I are weighed on the balances, what will God find? Will we be found wanting on His scales? In the Old Testament God spelled out clearly the standard by which He measured man—the Ten Commandments.

1. *Thou shalt have no other gods before me.*

Do we serve other gods? self? mammon? We can serve but one God.

What about money? Have we made it a god? We count it, envy those with more, lie for it, steal for it, quarrel about it, murder for it, gamble for it, and selfishly hoard it, yet are lonely if money is all we have.

2. *Thou shalt not make unto thee any graven image.*

Money is only one example of the "images" we worship. Another is television; how many hours spent in front of it could have been devoted to worthwhile projects? Another is golf.

The images we worship are all around us and are in our hearts where God should dwell. Many worship lust and pleasure, whiskey and drugs. Others bow before social position or political power. Anything we esteem or love more than God *is* our god. Will we be found wanting?

3. *Thou shalt not take the name of the Lord thy God in vain.*

Profanity is common today on the streets, in schools, farms, homes, courts, in movies and even on television. Pity the man who so little reverences God that he takes His name in vain.

4. *Remember the sabbath day, to keep it holy.*

The Sabbath has been called "the pause in time which indicates eternity," and "heaven's milestone along the highway of time."

Jesus said that the Sabbath was made for man, for man to rest and worship God.

Many who work seven days a week are compelled, but others—some of whom own businesses and could release their employees—are tyrants who have no use for God's laws. May God save us from making His holy day a working day, or a holiday of hunting, fishing, swimming, riding, excursions, movies, parties, games, and concerts.

God has never repealed this law, and if we disregard it, we will decay spiritually and invoke God's wrath.

5. *Honour thy father and thy mother: that thy days may be long upon the land which the Lord thy God giveth thee.*

Nothing is more contemptible than to dishonor your parents. Are you ashamed of their wrinkled faces, hands that show hard work, bent backs, old clothing, white hair, and slow step? Those are jewels in a crown of love for you. A daughter or son can dishonor a mother and father by a reckless, mean, and sinful life. Would you want their epitaph to read: "Their hearts were broken by a wayward son (daughter)"?

6. *Thou shalt not kill.*

Some ways of killing are more respectable than shooting,

poisoning, cutting, or hitting over the head with an axe. Few of us would resort to such extremes, but many daily kill our husbands or wives by slow torture: neglect, unkindness, unfaithfulness, cruelty, and drunkenness. Would you want your spouse's epitaph to read, "Killed by an unfaithful partner"?

7. *Thou shalt not commit adultery.*

We shrink from discussing this commandment, but ours is a sex-conscious age. God voices sternest disapproval of the misuse of sex.

The vilest man is the one who ruins another's home; the vilest woman, no matter how fair of face, is the one who diverts a husband's affection from his wife.

We have utterly disregarded this commandment. In Matthew 5:28 Jesus said "that whosoever looketh on a woman to lust after her hath committed adultery with her already in his heart."

Are you found wanting here?

8. *Thou shalt not steal.*

The dictionary says that to steal is "to take money or property from another without rendering to the other a sufficient equivalent in property or money return."

In other words, we steal if we misrepresent the quality of certain goods, if we buy goods and do not give the value received, if we pay employees less than an honest wage, if we shirk work, or if we gamble. More of us steal than we realize.

9. *Thou shalt not bear false witness against thy neighbour.*

"Bearing witness" in this context does not mean testifying in court. It means speaking evil of a person, passing on information that is false, exaggerated, or distorted. You have borne false witness if you knowingly tell a lie about another, or if you slander and gossip.

I have as much respect for a thief who deliberately steals a man's fortune as I have for the one who steals a man's good reputation. The Bible says, "Thou shalt not go up and down as a talebearer among thy people."

Three ways to keep from breaking this law are; (1) never believe anything you hear about another unless you can verify it; (2) that which you are compelled to believe keep to yourself unless duty demands that it be told; (3) when you must tell it, tell it accurately.

10. *Thou shalt not covet.*

Covetousness is the unlawful desire for what does not belong to you. This includes not only your neighbor's house, wife, servants, ox, or ass, which the Bible mentions, but also his swimming pool, fine car, high position, or wealth. Covetousness is closely related to greed.

The Final Command

God gave these commandments to the people of Israel in Old Testament times. Jesus gave us a new and greater commandment, one which summarizes the earlier ones: "Thou shalt love the Lord thy God with all thy heart, and with all thy soul, and with all thy mind. This is the first and great commandment" (Matt. 22:37, 38).

In George Macdonald's *Malcolm,* the dying marquis sends for the schoolmaster, Mr. Graham. The schoolmaster knows the marquis well and begins with caution:

"Are you satisfied with yourself, my lord?"

"No, by God!"

"You would be better?"

"Yes; but how is a poor devil to get out of this infernal scrape?"

"Keep the commandments."

"That's it, of course; but there's no time!"

"If there were but time to draw another breath, there would be time to begin."

"How am I to begin? Which am I to begin with?"

"Believe on the Lord Jesus Christ, and thou shalt be saved."

If we are weighed in the balances, will we be found wanting? Of course! Yet there is a way out, for Jesus said, "If thou shalt confess with thy mouth the Lord Jesus, and shalt believe in thine heart that God hath raised him from the dead, thou shalt be saved."

When the Sun Shone at Midnight / 5

John 3:4

Nicodemus saith unto him, How can a man be born when he is old? . . .

What do you consider the essential experience of the Christian life? Leo Tolstoy wrote in middle age:

> Five years ago I came to believe in Christ and my life suddenly changed. . . . It happened to me as it happens to a man who goes out on some business and on the way suddenly decides that the business is unnecessary and returns home. All that was on his right is now on his left, and all that was on his left is now on his right. The former wish, to go as far as possible from home, has changed into a wish to be as near as possible to it. The direction of my life and my desires became different, and good and evil changed places.

For Tolstoy, the essential Christian experience was conversion: the turning from one loyalty to another, the reversal of values, the bisection of life into two periods—"before" and "after."

The secret of Christian experience lies in becoming not an improved person but a new person, altogether different from the person you once were. When Nicodemus, the wealthy Pharisee, came by night to discuss religion with Jesus, the Master described this change with a figure of speech. "Except a man be born again, he cannot see the kingdom of God." A man must, figuratively speaking, die and begin life anew if God is to save him and give a sense of eternal security.

Where is the man who has never reviewed his life and wished that he could, by some miracle, go back and start over? Who has not felt dissatisfied with his pattern of living? Who has not yearned with Omar Khayyam to "smash this sorry scheme of things entire"?

We should like very much to start fresh, but it seems impossible. Our habits, thoughts, behavior patterns, failures, prejudices seem fixed, congealed. We wish it could be different, but figure it is too late to change now.

Formed, Deformed, Reformed

Nicodemus' question might have been rhetorical—not a question at all but a slightly sarcastic denial: "How can a man be born when he is old?"

Many people, realists all, say "you just can't change human nature." An old proverb says: "Sow a thought, and you reap an act; sow an act, and you reap a habit; sow a habit, and you reap a character; sow a character, and you reap a destiny." This proverb teaches that human nature cannot be changed, and many people believe it.

I do not. Let us consider the matter with open minds. A leopard can't change his spots, but man, who is made in the image of God, is more than animal.

Students of psychology agree that human nature can be changed. One preacher said: "When you tell me that human nature cannot be changed, I am constrained to reply that, in the light of experience, human nature is the only thing that *can* be changed."

Psychology and psychiatry operate on the premise that a maladjusted human being made wretched by a collection of repressions and complexes, through careful analysis can be changed into a new creature. He can start life over again with new self-confidence and self-reliance.

Many universities maintain schools of social work, training professionals to help the delinquent, the degenerate, and the criminal to change, to overcome heredity and early environment, and to become useful, self-respecting members of society.

But if human nature can change for the better, it can also change for the worse. Someone who was once cheerful, idealistic, and brave becomes callous, cynical, and self-centered. Israel's King Saul was a classic example. In his youth he was handsome, tall, and fair, graced by modesty and admired throughout the land for his bravery and ability to lead. On the throne he became consumed by jealousy, subject to fits of brooding melancholy and neurotic rage, mistrusting his own loyal servants and family.

Scientists of mental phenomena tell us that, of all living creatures, man is the most plastic, his nature most subject to change. Though we may argue it, it remains a well-authenticated fact that people are reborn, that human personality flowing in one direction can suddenly reverse itself, going from "formed, to deformed, to reformed." We *can* be changed, for better or for worse.

But How?

Nicodemus did not dispute Christ's claim that life in God should begin with conversion and rebirth. He did not deny that, if men would fulfill the image of God, they must change radically and decisively. He merely asked, "How can a man be born when he is old?" He did not doubt his need of the new birth; perhaps he thought it impractical. Born again? How could that be? He was old; his life was almost over. Once it might have been possible, but now? How could he be born again?

Nicodemus' interest was probably genuine; maybe he warmed up to the idea of conversion and became really intrigued by it.

Isn't this all Jesus asks? An open-minded interest? He will not bully us into the kingdom; He constrains us to obey with His winsome character, His magnetic leadership, His reasonable teaching, His suffering love upon the cross, His powerful presence in our hearts. He only asks that men be impartial, that they forsake the assumption that what He says is either wrong or insignificant. He asks only that we lay aside our biases and listen with open minds.

Nicodemus didn't have to look far for the answer to his question. In the very house in which he met Jesus were men of all ages sleeping as peacefully as newborn babes; they had died to their old lives and started over again as children of God.

Down in Jericho was a man named Zaccheus, a Jew who had been a tax collector, an unscrupulous little quisling feared and hated by his people. Now he was known for his astonishing integrity and kindliness, and for his dedication to returning money he had once collected fraudulently.

Up in Magdala was a woman named Mary, an excitingly lovely woman whose body had been her stock in trade, salable to the highest bidder. Now she was living a life of astonishing purity and modesty, dedicated to uplifting the very people who had exploited and despised her.

These men and women had been born when they were old —living proof that human nature can be changed. And all of them were staring Nicodemus in the face.

What was their secret?

They had met Jesus, who looked at them with love and understanding, forgiving them with the eyes of God, whose own pure presence awakened their sleeping impulses to nobility and grandeur, and whose friendship drew them from the gutters of shame and cynicism to the firm road of self-respect and hope.

The story of Christianity is replete with evidence that human nature may be changed.

How can a man be born when he is old? There is no stereotyped answer. It happens in different ways, it does not conform to an unvarying pattern. William James described some of the ways in which men meet God, in a great book entitled *Varieties of Religious Experience*.

I doubt seriously if any two people are ever reborn in exactly the same way. I have heard many thrilling testimonies, and while they have had many elements in common, no two have been exactly alike. They differ as human beings differ.

Many feel that they have been saved in a sudden, spectacular experience; the hour, day, and place will never be forgotten. Others cannot name the time and place, but they know that once they were lost and now they are found. They were blind, but now they see. What matters is not *how* salvation comes but *that* it comes.

Thomas Chalmers, perhaps the greatest Scotsman since John

Knox, regarded the church in his early years as unworthy of all the devotion and intellectual vigor it demanded. But some time later, he realized that he had had a profound religious experience, although he could not describe or date it; he realized that he had laid all his great learning upon God's altar. Christ and the church now claimed all of him, and he said to a Scottish assembly on one occasion: "What, sir, is the object of mathematical science? Magnitude and the proportions of magnitude. But then, sir, I had forgotten two magnitudes. I thought not of the littleness of time . . . I recklessly thought not of the greatness of eternity!"

We may well ask ourselves, Have we been born again, or have we substituted something else for it? Have we exchanged a pleasant worship of the church for a new birth in the Holy Spirit? Are we new persons, inside and out?

Jesus had no simple answer to Nicodemus' question. Men cannot regulate God's redeeming grace. "The wind bloweth where it listeth, and thou hearest the sound thereof, but canst not tell whence it cometh, and whither it goeth: so is every one that is born of the Spirit" (John 3:8).

Of one thing we may be sure: as human nature has been altered for 1900 years by scientific stimulation, so for 1900 years those who have been influenced by Christ's friendship and love have totally different personalities. Armed with new loves, new hates, and new aims, they are prepared to contradict what they hitherto affirmed and to affirm what they hitherto contradicted.

This, then, is the answer to Nicodemus' question: A man can be born when he is old through his relationship with Jesus Christ.

Jesus Christ Is the Answer

Suppose Nicodemus asked this question in still another way —with passionate, profound yearning, as though this were the supreme secret, the pearl of great price which he had been seeking all of his life. "I am tired of my life, tired of the person I am, tired of this losing battle between my ideals and my weak, sinful nature. Spiritually I ought to be erased from the book of life as though I had never been born."

Is it possible to both yearn for and not really want this essential experience of the Christian life?

Imagine an arthritic cripple who for twenty years has been bedridden. A miracle healer comes to him and says compassionately, "I shall make you well. I shall straighten those twisted limbs and restore life to that useless body. Rise from your bed and go out into the world." But the arthritic has thrived on misery, self-pity, and the sympathy of others for too long. He answers, "No."

Just so, many people have become used to the misery of moral and spiritual paralysis, and though they may wish for the strength and freedom that healing would bring, they lack the courage to accept it when it is offered. Yet, all they need do is accept it!

New birth is not something you can do; only God can do it. You do not have the power to re-create life any more than the power to create it. The secret is Jesus Christ. "If any man be in Christ, he is a new creature: old things are passed away; behold, all things are become new" (II Cor. 5:17).

An old Dutch fable tells of three tulip bulbs, *No*, *Yes*, and *Maybe*, which lived at the bottom of a bulb tin, clothed in silky, brown garments, content to be round and fat. When autumn came, they fell to discussing the destiny of tulip bulbs.

No said, "I shall stay in my snug corner of the bin. That there is any other life for tulip bulbs I deny. Besides, I am satisfied with things as they are." And he rolled over in his corner to sleep the winter away.

Maybe said, "I am not satisfied with things as they are. I feel that there is a better life than the life I now have. I feel something inside me which I must achieve, and I believe that I can achieve it." So he squeezed and squeezed himself and ended up in frustration.

Then *Yes* said, "I have been told that we can do nothing of ourselves, but that the good Lord will fulfill our destiny if we put ourselves in His power."

So one day a hand reached down into the bin, groping for tulip bulbs. *Yes* gave himself to the hand and was buried in the earth throughout the long winter months. Meanwhile, *No* and *Maybe* shriveled away to uselessness, but when spring came, *Yes* burst forth with all the richness and loveliness of new life.

"If any man be in Christ, he is a new creature: old things are passed away; behold, all things are become new"!

The Land of Beginning Again / 6

Romans 12:2

. . . be not conformed to this world: but be ye transformed by the renewing of your mind . . .

Louise Fletcher Tarkington has expressed the heartfelt desire of millions of people:

I wish that there were some wonderful place
Called the Land of Beginning Again.

Is there such a land? Is it possible to move backwards? Huxley tells us, "The unseen opponent in the great game of life, while scrupulously fair, will allow no back moves, and makes us pay in full for every blunder." Is he right?

Even those of us whose faith has been strong have at times been doubtful and suspicious, and wondered if a back move is possible. Surely it would be enormously difficult to begin again.

I hear the bitter cry of John B. Gough: "The scars remain! scars never to be eradicated, never to be removed in this life. I have been plucked like a brand from the burning; but the scar of the fire is on me!"

Many of us have become so "conformed" to the world, so entangled in it and enmeshed in its ways, that we think "Perhaps God can save some, but not me." Our systems are too poisoned by greed, by drink, by lust, by envy, by indifference, by failure, to make any back moves.

George Macdonald, in the story of *Wilfred Cumbermede*, puts in words how many of us feel:

> "Do you know, Wilfred, I once shot a little bird—for no good, but just to shoot at something. I knew it was wrong, yet I drew the trigger. It dropped, a heap of ruffled feathers. I shall never get that little bird out of my head. And the worst of it is that to all eternity I can never make any atonement."
>
> "But God will forgive you, Charley!"
>
> "What do I care for that," he rejoined almost fiercely,"when the little bird cannot forgive me?"

Past sins make back moves difficult. Heaven is merciful, but earth may find it hard to entertain kind thoughts of us. And, unhappily, the wreckage men have wrought is not always confined to a heap of ruffled feathers. Suppose, instead of little birds, our own flesh and blood were to rise up in judgment against us?

Is the cheerless philosophy of Omar Khayyam true?

> The Moving Finger writes; and having writ,
> Moves on: nor all your piety nor wit
> Shall lure it back to cancel half a line,
> Nor all your tears wash out a word of it.

There Is Such a Land

We may have doubted, but in our better moments we have known that there is a wonderful place called the land of beginning again. Some of us have been there and know it firsthand; we who have been marred by sin have seen our sins vanish as a dark cloud from the face of the sky—erased, forgotten, cast out behind God's back to the depths of the sea. It is as though we had never been wicked at all. The gospel offers us a magnificent back move.

Your conscience says, "You need not be the way you are." Heaven answers, "No man need stay where he is."

The fires of conscience burn hottest when a person hears its voice and tries to ignore the second. One physician has said: "Every physician who has much to do with nervous troubles and emotional disorders soon comes to recognize that thousands of well-meaning individuals are suffering from mental torture and various nervous disorders as the result of overworking the conscience. The voice of conscience can be an acute problem *if we do not listen to it.*"

That you need not remain where you are is true in many areas of life.

Doctors say that you need not be ill, and scientific medicine is constantly discovering preventions and cures for more diseases.

Illiteracy and ignorance are also unnecessary. Education is trying to remedy these problems. Adult education has proved that you can teach old dogs new tricks.

Desert areas and unfruitful valleys need not remain unproductive. Irrigation has done wonders for Israel and Peru.

Change is possible. One would never have guessed that the young Gandhi of London, who dressed smartly, danced beautifully, and played social games, would become Mahatma Gandhi of India—"that young fellow who turned out to be the toothless, half-naked ascetic living on goat's milk, holding in his frail hands the spiritual destinies of India, and almost single-handedly forced the British Empire to reverse its policy." But it happened!

The Bible Speaks

The Old Testament, especially the prophetic books, says much about back moves.

In the beautiful story of the potter who took a marred vessel and remade it, God asks, "O house of Israel, cannot I do with you as this potter?" (Jer. 18:6) And He made Israel anew. Cannot He do the same for you?

Joel reports an historic and unprecedented plague of locusts which devastated the land: the sun was darkened, the fields and vineyards reduced to a howling wilderness, business paralyzed, the sacrifices in the Temple suspended. In the midst of national calamity the prophet cried, "Fear not, O land; be glad and rejoice: for the Lord will do great things. . . . I will restore to you the years that the locust hath eaten" (2:21, 25). The sun shone, the vines bore luscious clusters, grass abounded for the cattle, and the valleys produced golden crops. The Temple was crowded with devout worshipers. The years that the locusts had eaten had been restored. The message to you, Sinner, is that, when you are down and out, God will restore to you the years that time and sin have eaten.

The New Testament also says something about the land of beginning again.

Paul, who vividly illustrates the possibility of starting over, also illustrates the constant battle waged within anyone who makes a new beginning: "I delight in the law of God after the inward man: But I see another law in my members, warring against the law of my mind, and bringing me into captivity to the law of sin which is in my members" (Rom. 7:22, 23). Plato described the one engaged in such a battle as "driving a chariot with two horses, one white and disciplined, and the other black and fractious." And Goethe's Faust acknowledged that "two souls, alas, are lodged within my breast." This battle within us keeps us from becoming static, staid human beings; challenges us to grow and change, in freedom and love.

From Being to Becoming

Jesus discovered in Palestine a world like ours, full of unpromising people: the woman of Samaria who had had five husbands; the woman of the street who washed his feet; the woman who had committed adultery; prodigal sons like those in His parable; the dishonest public officials like Zaccheus; blunderers like Peter. They were "conformed" to this world, but Jesus "transformed" them. He sized them up, but He did not stop there. He changed them by looking at them in a new light, in terms of what they might become. What a teacher!

When Robert Louis Stevenson changed direction and became a young man with a purpose, he did not think he had guided himself, but that he had been guided by that "unknown steersman whom we call God."

When Keats read Spencer's *Faerie Queene*, he was transformed from a young lad without a vocation into an aspiring poet. He did not think he had changed himself, but that he had been changed, born from above by a vision of a world of beauty he had never before sensed.

You may not be able to change yourself, but Jesus can change you. He will lift you instead of making you lift yourself. This is His superiority to the moralists. Other religions tell the man in the ditch how to get out; Jesus reaches down and helps him out. If the man cooperates, he can help bring about the change.

Change, like sin, is an intimate and personal thing. Preaching is like holding an eyedropper of medicine out a window and dispensing one drop at a time into the street below, hoping that it will hit somebody in the right place; sinners do not simply step up and confess their sins. Yet each of us knows his own sins.

You who use profanity can change.

You with the terrible temper, the hysteria, the crazy capers—you are brutal, cruel, and spoiled, and you are ruining your life and your family's happiness, but you can change.

You who like Zaccheus have robbed the poor and cheated in business can change.

You who are enslaved by habits, habits that drive you mad if they go unsatisfied, habits that embitter you and threaten death itself if you don't sustain them, can break them!

You who are in sin! You who are lost! Your conscience says, "You need not be."

Hezekiah Butterworth wrote a poem about a bird that fell into a snare and broke a wing. The bird could never soar as high as it had,

> But the bird with the broken pinion
> Kept another from the snare,
> And the life that sin had stricken
> Raised another from despair.
> Each loss has its compensations.
> There is healing for every pain.
> Though the bird with the broken pinion
> Never soars so high again.

How does Jesus Christ transform us? By loving us with a love that will not let us go. Yes, love is the theme of Jesus' message. Love is the reason He died for us on the cross. It is the mightiest, most transforming, life-changing force in the world. Nothing is as powerful. That is why the cross breaks men's hearts. "Why," we wonder, "should He love me so?"

We can begin again if we will do it at the foot of the cross. If Jesus cared enough to die for you, must you not admit, "I know I need not be the way I am," and pray that "with God's grace I will not stay that way."

"Be not conformed to this world: but be ye transformed. . . ."

Living Can Be Sublime / 7

Philippians 1:21

For to me to live is Christ. . . .

When H. G. Wells lay on his deathbed in 1946, goes one account, he said to a visitor: "Don't bother me. Can't you see I'm busy dying?"

"Busy dying." Isn't that what we are all doing—dying physically day by day? Two or three days after birth the dying process begins, and just about the time we get ready to live, it's time to die.

This is not a cheerful thought, but even more tragic is that some of us are dying or dead, spiritually, and don't even know it.

What about you? Are you busy dying?

What would we be like if we were busy living? living as Jesus intended—more abundantly?

What shall we do with life in this stupendous age? Dickens' line, "It was the best of times, it was the worst of times," describes our own age as well as it did Victorian England. The changes in the last fifty years have been confounding, swift, and radical.

Yet this world is all we have, and if we are to make the most of it, we need to live for something, some ideal, some purpose. If there is no reason to life, there is no reason for life. It is soon over, and either we have lived fully or we haven't.

Your life is in your hands. Within certain limits it can be what you want it to be. What kind of life would you choose if you had your choice? If dreams were for sale, which would you buy? Would you live subsistently or sublimely? Would you be self-centered and self-seeking or selfless and self-giving? What would you do with your life?

A number of possibilities exist.

Five Alternatives

1. *You may run from life.* You may try to escape as Jonah did and as men still do, but you will never succeed: the world is round and you will keep returning to where you began.

I remember an antebellum home which through the years slowly decayed and rotted away, and as it did, the family retreated more and more to the inner rooms, dragging bits of furniture with them. Finally, there they sat, hugging themselves in the only room left, trying to ignore the disintegration all around them. They refused to repair the house with good will, or reinforce it with dedication, or reroof it with service, or install new windows with faith. Half the world is bleeding and needy, and they retreated into the innermost room, seeking comfort.

2. *You may also run with life.* You may run with the herd, huddle with the pack. You may coast instead of climb, drift instead of drive. But like a piece of deadwood floating downstream, you will leave no trace; no one will ever know that you lived.

Some people still consider the devil a monster with horns, a harpoon tail, and a wicked glitter in his eye. Whatever his appearance, the devil is active, aggressive, vindictive, unscrupulous, and organized in keeping us inert, doing nothing, and taking the line of least resistance.

To run with life is to succumb to the devil and drift.

3. *You may see life as a comedy and laugh at it.* Many think of life as a joke. They want to eat, drink, and make merry, lest the joke be on them and they die tomorrow. They seem unaware that they are already dead or dying.

4. *You may see life as a tragedy and cry over it.* A great circus was underway, the animals performing, the clowns entertaining. Large crowds were enjoying the merriment when a wisp of smoke

and a bit of flame suddenly brought pandemonium. Comedy turned to tragedy as the tent burned to the ground.

Life may become a tragedy overnight if we allow suffering and grief to drown us in despair.

5. *You may see life as a farce and sneer at it.* Some see life as a merry-go-round, a meaningless round of existence, monotonous, and amounting to nothing. They go round and round until dizzy, finally getting off two or three feet from where they got on. Life for them is an endless round of sleeping, working, and eating.

The Choice Is Ours

The point is, we make the choice; we view life as we wish to view it. We can view it in one of the ways mentioned or in a far better way. That way is to invest life with a plan, a purpose, a faith, and some discipline.

Montague, the English novelist, was one of a group of students at Oxford who heard Benjamin Jowett preach on life: "I have seen it set down in tables that the average length of life of a man of twenty-one is thirty-six years. He may hope for a little more, he may fear for a little less, but roughly speaking, it is thirty-six years. That is, 13,000 days. He is a shabby sort of fellow who wastes any part of those 13,000 days: a gentleman is the man who refuses to take out of life more than he puts into it."

The youths returned to their living quarters and did some figuring. They estimated that one third of those days are spent sleeping, one third making a living, and one third, or 4,333 days, making whatever contribution one can to mankind. They resolved to waste no more time, to use every minute. They took hold of life and did something with it; almost every man in that group distinguished himself in one field or another.

Of course, the best way to proceed is to commit our lives to One greater than any of us. Paul did this and said, "For to me to live is Christ." Life becomes sublime when dedicated to something greater than itself, when it seeks no reward. When we surrender our lives to God, we will discover that "he that loseth his life for my sake shall find it."

If we are to live full lives, we must have four things:

1. *A faith to live and die by,* a faith that satisfies the mind and sanctifies the heart. Faith is the "antiseptic of the soul," the disinfectant of fear. It makes us victors instead of victims.

2. *A philosophy of life.* Great men and civilizations would not have been great without a philosophy of life. Socrates' creed was "Know thyself." Rome's was "Control thyself." Judea's was "Give thyself." If we give ourselves and forgive others, we will fill our hearts with thanksgiving.

3. *A self fit to live with.* We must live with ourselves whether we like it or not. If we cannot live with ourselves in peace, we cannot live with others in peace. If we cannot accept ourselves, we will find it difficult to accept God's grace.

4. *A work fit to live for.* Great causes make great men. The world is full of great causes, aching needs which cry for help. We are here not only to make a living but also to make a life; the only way to do this is to give ourselves to others.

James L. S. Dunlop, a Canadian Air Force sergeant, crashed to his death on October 11, 1941. Based in England, he had written to his parents a letter that was to be mailed only if he failed to return from one of his flights. The letter said: "If there is any message which the coming generations should have from mine, let it be a message from one of us who have fought and died to make future generations of human beings possible. Let the message be this: 'We have cleared the site and laid the foundations. You build!' "

Are we building?

Are we living?

"I have set before you life and death . . . therefore choose life, that both thou and thy seed may live" (Deut. 30:19).

Does Death End All? / 8

Job 14:14

If a man die, shall he live again? . . .

When the gospel was first taken to Britain, a crowd of eager listeners gathered in the court of Edwin, King of Northumbria, to hear the teachers of the new religion.

After some discussion, a grim and bearded earl rose and asked, "Can the new religion tell us what lies beyond death?"

That question is older than Job. Even Job wondered in agony whether the grave was really the end. If it was, he thought, then life is a tangled web of injustice and wrong, and no wise and good God is at the heart of things. He passionately desired assurance of life beyond the grave.

When a man dies, will he live again?

Of all aspects of religion, I have been most perplexed by immortality. Early in life I was told about everlasting life, and almost as early I doubted it. I found it very difficult to believe that I would live forever, yet deep in my heart was the ineradicable instinct that said I would.

I turned to the world for an answer.

Three Answers

Science told me that future life is not only possible, it might even be probable. The evidence of the indestructibility of matter and the conservation of energy is too strong for any scientist to deny the possibility of life after death. Is it likely that senseless atoms of matter endure and the living soul perishes? Science does not veto immortality; it leaves the door open.

Philosophy told me that man's sense of this life's incompleteness demands another stage of life. Man's superiority to beasts lay in his conscious powers of reason. The beast, lacking a moral conscience, demands nothing beyond. But man's conscious reason tells him he is part of something more than he finds in this world.

Robert Louis Stevenson described this longing in these words:

> Whatever crazy sorrow saith,
> No life that breathes with human breath
> Has ever truly longed for death.
> This life whereof our nerves are scant,
> Oh, life, not death, for which we pant,
> More life and fuller that we want.

If future life is permitted by science and demanded by philosophy, it is confirmed and uncovered by the revelation of Jesus Christ. Uncertainty is banished, darkness becomes light. The *gospel* told me that Jesus Christ provides immortality. "In my Father's house are many mansions: if it were not so, I would have told you." More important, Jesus teaches that this life and the next are of a piece—living and dying and living again. "I give unto them eternal life; and they shall never perish, neither shall any man pluck them out of my hand. My Father, which gave them me, is greater than all; and no man is able to pluck them out of my Father's hand."

Knowing is one dimension of life, *believing* is another. I *believe* in immortality because I believe in *man, God,* and *Christ.*

Faith in Man

I believe in immortality because I believe in man—his universal instinct for immortality, and his value.

In the words of Henry Ward Beecher, "I believe in immortality because I feel it in my bones." The same thing that tells the birds to go north and south tells man that he is made to live. Centuries before Abraham, men believed in life after death. Some of the most cultivated minds this world has known have believed in it, unable to suppress the instinct. The ancient Egyptians embalmed the bodies of their dead and put them in tombs for immortality. Allusions to immortality are scattered throughout the Old Testament. The instincts of man, the crown and goal of creation, can be trusted.

Because man is the crown of creation, he is too valuable to die. Shall a person not outlive the bed upon which he sleeps? Shall a man not outlive the things he makes with his hands? Will man end in a black hole in the ground? If so, this world is irrational.

Some elephants have lived three hundred years; is man less valuable than an elephant? An oak lives for hundreds of years; shall man cease to live at three score and ten? Tennyson wrote, "I know transplanted human worth will bloom to profit, otherwhere." I believe in immortality because man is too valuable to die.

Love testifies that man is too important to die. A baby taken from a home by death is too valuable never to be seen again. "Endless love implies endless living."

Faith in God

I believe in immortality because I believe in God.

If there is no immortality, there is no God. Is it conceivable that the eternal Father would call into being countless generations of human personalities all doomed to speedy extinction? The average life of man is scarcely more than seventy years; does God weary of us by the time we have reached three-score and ten? If God has a Father-love for human beings, and humans have such a limited existence, would not God be in perpetual bereavement? Would it not render His own existence a continuous tragedy? Would Father-love sweep generations of men into extinction, merely to make room for others to appear and play their part? If God has no higher end for us than fertilizer for the lives of those who follow us, could we call Him "Father"?

Jesus teaches that God is love. If Jesus is right and God is immortal love, then wouldn't He give immortal life to His children? Only a human soul that is immortal could satisfy divine love.

Equity demands immortality. Where is equity on earth, you ask? Man longs for justice but sees little of it in the world. Someday, somewhere, all inequalities and injustices will be rectified. There must be a life beyond the grave.

Immortality is essential to progress. A poet like Keats dies with his poetry in his head; a boy with high ambition dies in war with all of his aspirations unrealized; a man on the verge of a great invention or medical discovery succumbs to cancer. If there is no sequel, progress for men and nations is impossible. All that we can learn in a lifetime is but an atom compared to what there is to learn in a future world. *Jonathan Livingston Seagull* was one man's vision of what a dreamer might do if immortal. Man is equipped for eternity. Shall one overequipped for this life be squashed like an insect after a few brief years?

I believe in immortality because I believe in God.

Faith in Christ

I also believe in immortality because I believe in Christ. "Our Saviour Jesus Christ . . . hath abolished death, and hath brought life and immortality to light through the gospel" (II Tim. 1:10).

I believe in immortality because of what Christ was and is. He didn't argue immortality, He declared it. The doctrine of immortality is woven together with that of redemption; you cannot have one without the other. He promised His disciples immortality: "I give unto them eternal life."

Had man been mortal like the leaves of the tree and the grass of the field, he would have been unworthy of Christ's sacrifice, a sacrifice made not for creatures on their way to dust, but for spirits who must presently meet God. Either Jesus died for immortal souls, or He was lured to the cross by a false light glimmering in mockery over a realm of universal death.

I believe in immortality because Christ arose from the dead. His triumph over death brings immortality into the full blaze of the noonday sun. Illuminated by the gospel of Christ, immortality becomes supremely desirable. Do you shrink from immortality?

Are you afraid of it? Do you have a host of unanswered questions? We all have questions concerning the afterlife. Let's take a look at some of them.

Five Questions

1. *What sort of body shall we have?*

"But some man will say, How are the dead raised up? and with what body do they come?"

We shrink from the thought of life without a body; it leaves us with a sense of incompleteness. Yet the Bible is clear on some aspects of death. "God giveth it a body as it hath pleased him. . . . it is sown a natural body; it is raised a spiritual body. . . . flesh and blood cannot inherit the kingdom of God; neither doth corruption inherit incorruption. Behold, I shew you a mystery; we should not all sleep, but we shall all be changed."

When John Quincy Adams was eighty, he met an old friend on the streets of Boston who said, "Good morning, and how is John Quincy Adams today?"

"John Quincy Adams is well, sir; quite well, I thank you. But the house in which he lives at present is becoming dilapidated. It is tottering upon its foundations. Time and seasons have nearly destroyed it. Its walls are much shattered, and it trembles with every wind. The old tenement is becoming almost uninhabitable, and I think John Quincy Adams will have to move out soon; but he himself is quite well, sir; quite well."

Yes, the body is sown in corruption but is raised incorruptible. It is sown in dishonor but will be raised in glory. It is sown in weakness but will be raised in power. It is sown a natural body but will be raised a spiritual body.

The spiritual body shall fulfill the desires of the spiritual man. We are shaping the spiritual body now; as a life of sin brings a body of sin, so the life of Christ brings the body of Christ.

2. *Is there consciousness beyond death?*

If we are to believe the Scriptures, yes. Moses and Elijah came down and talked with Jesus shortly before His death. Paul spoke of departing and being with Christ. Jesus said, "To day shalt thou be with me in paradise."

Beyond a doubt our loved ones have gone to a full, vivid, conscious life in memory, thought, love, and character.

3. *Do those who pass into the great beyond remember those they leave behind?*

If they are conscious, they will retain their memories. Lazarus remembered Dives; Dives remembered the old home and the brothers he grew up with. Our risen Lord remembered all the past. The writer of Hebrews believed that all who have gone before are watching us: "Seeing we also are compassed about with so great a cloud of witnesses, let us lay aside every weight, and the sin which doth so easily beset us, and let us run with patience the race that is set before us. . ."

This poses an obvious difficulty, of course: how can those in heaven be happy if they know of the sorrows that scourge us, the crosses we carry, the sins and mistakes and follies that beset us? How can they enjoy the bliss of heaven?

There is no easy reply, but perhaps they see more clearly than do we that "our light affliction, which is but for a moment, worketh for us a far more exceeding and eternal weight of glory."

4. *Can they serve us?*

> Ever near us, though unseen,
> The dear immortal spirits tread;
> For all the boundless universe
> Is life—there are no dead.

Much leads us to believe that they who have been near, who have known and loved us, must still serve us in some useful way. The Scriptures tell us that angels are "ministering spirits, sent forth to minister for them who shall be heirs of salvation." If angels, why not also our loved ones and friends?

"The angel stood to offer the prayers of all the saints upon the golden altar," says John in Revelation. What that means it is hard to say, but possibly the "prayers of all the saints" are the prayers of the blessed dead on our behalf. Can you imagine that those who loved us so deeply and agonizingly on earth would cease their prayer and service in a realm where they at last have power to serve? The silent hosts of those we call dead are all about us. They watch. Perhaps they pray.

5. *Can we serve them?*

I can think of at least one way in which we can. As Tennyson said in "Morte d'Arthur," "More things are wrought by prayer than this world dreams of."

Many saints, by praying with and for those in the spirit world, with loved ones real and near, have been able to conquer that poignant separation which is so much a part of bereavement.

I am not calling for prayers on behalf of those in purgatory, nor for spiritualism. I am saying that, if Dives, suffering in torment, prayed that someone should go to his five brothers and win them, it is reasonable to think that a godly mother or father who prayed for a son or daughter while living might want someone to carry on those prayers after they are gone.

Whatever the answers to these five questions, we know this: whether *life* is the end or the beginning is determined by our relationship to Jesus Christ; whether *death* is the end or the beginning is also determined by our relationship to Jesus Christ. Death has no magic to change us; earthly life determines our futures.

How we live determines whether we can say, "For to me . . . to die is gain." We can say this only when for us to live is Christ.

In the light of the gospel, immortality summons us all to repent and obey Christ while we are yet mortal. It compels us to view our present lives from the vantage point of eternity. Illuminated by Christ's gospel, immortality mightily inspires us to live worthily; it gives new meaning and greater value to our little day of life. Every bit of good we do in this world will follow us into the next. We build now for the future, so we should build well. John Greenleaf Whittier said in the poem "Eternal Goodness":

> Within the maddening maze of things,
> And tossed by storm and flood,
> To one fixed trust my spirit clings:
> I know that God is good.
> . . . .
> I know not where His islands lift
> Their fronded palms in air;
> I only know I cannot drift
> Beyond His love and care.

The Dignity of Man / 9

Psalm 8:4

What is man, that thou are mindful of him? . . .

Imagine a young man stretched out on a fragrant grassy hillside in the late evening, enjoying the clean mountain air and the clear dark sky. The beauty of the heavens overwhelms him and he silently asks himself, With the vastness of the heavens and the number of stars above, who am I that God should care for me?

The psalmist asked the same question hundreds of years ago. What indeed is man?

The Crown of Creation

Man is the crown and goal of divine creation.

From the lowest to the highest, God created the world: heaven and earth, light and darkness, day and night, sea and land, grass and flower, beast and bird. Then He said: "Let us make man in our image, after our likeness: and let him have dominion over the fish of the sea, and over the fowl of the air, and over the cattle, and over all the earth. . . . So God created man in his own image, in the image of God created he him; male and female created he them." All the lower stages were designed to serve the higher, and God chose man—the sum of all the lower stages—for a companion.

Some people feel that ancestry is everything; Oliver Wendell Holmes believed that a man's value was determined a hundred years before his birth. Yet, no matter how many noble or ignoble ancestors you may have had, we all have a common ancestry, one common Father. Each man can claim a Godly heritage. "God . . . hath made of one blood all nations."

Man's Uniqueness

Man is a unique creation in many ways.

First, he is the only creature with a *soul.* As frail as he is physically, his soul makes him supreme on earth. As one man observed, "When God made the world He used His power, but when He made man, He used Himself." He breathed into us the very breath of His life.

Second, man is also the only creature who can *reason.* William Shakespeare wrote: "What a piece of work is man! How noble in reason! How infinite in faculties! in form, how express and admirable! in action, how like an angel! in apprehension, how like a god! the beauty of the world! the paragon of animals!" And Pascal said, "Man is but a reed, the feeblest thing in nature; but he is a reed that thinks. An exhalation, a drop of water, suffice to destroy him. But were the universe to crush him, man is yet nobler than the universe; for he knows that he dies, and the universe, even in prevailing against him, knows not its power."

Third, man is the only creature who can be called the *child of God.* Jesus knew the deepest meaning of manhood. He knew that man was more than a product of nature. He took for granted that we were different from the plants and the animals; "Consider the lilies of the field," He exhorted us. They know not what they are, but you know, and you can draw on the lesson of their lower beauty in your higher life. Regard the birds of the air; they are dumb and dependent upon divine bounty, but you are conscious objects of divine care. Are you not of more value than the sparrows, whom God loves? Can you not sense the thrilling power of Jesus' high doctrine of humanity?

The Bible calls the stars and the beasts of the field God's works, but it calls man God's child. No other creature on earth can rise high enough to call God Father; only man has that privilege. A Hebrew poet said of man, "Thou hast made him a little lower than the angels, and hast crowned him with glory and honour."

We know that all men are of infinite value to God because Jesus spent most of His life among the poorest, the humblest of mankind . . . peasants, fishermen, children. He crowned with the crown of life all who would accept Him.

Fourth, man is the only creature with a *moral conscience*. He has a sense of right and wrong, a sense of guilt. The animal murders his prey and licks the blood from his paws; then goes his way untroubled, something man cannot do. His crime haunts him. He suffers biting remorse. The blood will not wash off.

> . . . no torture that the poets fain,
> Can match the fierce, unutterable pain
> He feels, who day and night, devoid of rest,
> Carries his own accuser in his breast.

Fifth, man is the only creature capable of *worship*. He is capable of communing with God and is incurably religious. No matter where he is, no matter how far removed from civilization and the light of the gospel, he worships deity in some fashion. Man has an enormous spiritual capacity to climb the stairway to God.

Finally, man is the only creature that is *immortal*.

> Dust thou art, to dust returnest,
> Was not spoken of the soul.

Man was created in the image of an immortal God. If man is capable of reflecting on divine holiness, he is capable of eternity. The idea of immortality permeates Jesus' teaching, and He died that man might enjoy immortality.

Why Believe in Man?

Materialism, commercialism, crowding, and debased views of human nature dominate our age. Never have we needed more to believe in the dignity of man. Only this will keep us from losing heart when confronted with the hatefulness, wickedness, and guilt of man. While man was created the glory of the universe, he is capable of being the scandal of creation. The most glorious of God's creatures may become the most inglorious. A Hebrew prophet said: "They are all gone out of the way, they are together become unprofitable; there is none that doeth good, no, not one. Their throat is an open sepulchre; with their tongues they have used deceit; the poison of asps is under their lips: Whose mouth is full of cursing and bitterness: Their feet are swift to shed blood: Destruction and misery are in their ways: And the way of peace have they not known: There is no fear of God before their eyes."

Given all we have learned, shouldn't human nature be better now than it was six thousand years ago? But is it? Every crime ever committed in the past has been committed in our age. Inhumanity is on the rampage, demon tormenting demon.

Anybody who thinks sin no longer exists is a fool, even if we don't hear much about it nowadays. Sin is real. It is the enemy and destroyer of mankind. It mars the divine image, ruins the glorious temple of God. It drags the company of God down to the company of swine. It brings misery and despair, strife and cruelty, murder and war, vice and shame. We need to hate sin as God hates it because it ruins His noblest creation.

Were it not for a high conception of manhood, poor, depraved, guilty, sinful human beings would be without hope.

The gospel tells us that a marred vessel can be remolded. A fallen man can be reconciled to God. The image of God may reflect divine holiness in heart and life. Man may rise up and be like God. There is hope if we respond to the Father's love. The sinner may be the man God wants him to be.

The restoration of forgotten art is a work of tedious love, but not half as difficult as the work Christ does in the hearts of men. He came to restore the likeness of God in man, to uncover the divine image. No human being has so marred God's image within that Christ cannot restore it.

A high conception of manhood helps us love and appreciate our fellows. Sometimes they are hard to love; some are so unlovely, so unattractive, so contemptible, so offensive. We shrink back, not wanting to be contaminated. Sometimes it seems that none is worthy of trust and love, and we want to despise and hate mankind.

But Jesus teaches us that love, not hate, is the light of life, the hope of the world. Christ died for all, and if every man is valuable to Him; can we strive for less? We love not what man is, but what man may become. "He which converteth the sinner from the error of his way shall save a soul from death, and hide a multitude of sins."

A belief in the dignity of man encourages us to live up to that dignity. At times we forget it and live as if there were no God, no future life, no soul within us. We concentrate on our earthly ambitions and pleasures and ignore and despise the high meaning of manhood. We forget the meaning of character. Horace Greeley wrote: "Fame is vapor; popularity is an accident; riches take wings; they who cheer today may curse tomorrow. One thing endures . . . character."

Wanted: A man to fill the gaps between God and man.

Wanted: A man with muscles like straps of steel, with will like iron, integrity and character unassailable, bottomless, summitless.

Wanted: Men who want to be saved from sin.

Wanted: Men who love Jesus Christ.

Or, in the words of J. G. Holland:

> God give us men! The time demands
> Strong minds, strong hearts, true faith
> and willing hands—
> Men whom the lust of office does not kill;
> Men whom the spoil of office cannot buy;
> Men who possess opinions and a will;
> Men who have honor; men who will not lie;
> Men who can stand before a demagogue
> And damn his treacherous flatteries without winking,
> Tall men, sun-crowned, who live above the fog
> In public duty and in private thinking.
> For while the rabble with their thumb-worn creeds,
> Their large professions and their little deeds,
> Mingle in selfish strife, lo! Freedom weeps!
> Wrong rules the land, and waiting justice sleeps!

Let us live with dignity and mirror the image of the Almighty God who created us.

Does Anybody Care? / 10

Psalm 142:4

. . . no man cared for my soul.

When David was being hunted like a partridge by a jealous king, he hid in a cave and poured out his heart to God. He was in great danger, pursued by an enemy, forsaken by friends, alone, trapped, with no way to escape. Those with him were unable to help; those who were able did not care. "I looked on my right hand, and beheld, but there was no man that would know me: refuge failed me; no man cared for my soul." As do most men in trouble, David fell back into the arms of God: "I cried unto thee, O Lord: I said, Thou art my refuge and my portion in the land of the living" (Ps. 142:5).

It is sad indeed that any man in any place at any time in history could truthfully say, "No man cared for my soul." Yet we know that countless thousands can. No man cares whether they are Christian or heathen, on the right side or the wrong, saved or lost, good or bad; whether they die in peace and triumph or waste and terror; whether they live in a world of love and hope or a world of sin, failure, defeat, remorse. So many persons lost and nobody cares!

Probably all of us feel at times that nobody cares, that this is a lonely world. We crave sympathy, companionship, friendship. We feel lonely, forsaken, forgotten. Loneliness is human. Even Jesus cried out, "My God, my God, why?"

How many times in our misery, we fall back on God, pouring out our hearts to Him for lack of human love, sympathy, and fellowship. "I cried unto the Lord with my voice, . . . and shewed before him my trouble." Think of the times you have called upon God in moments of despair and loneliness. You find yourself asking, "Does anybody really care?"

What We Do Care About

Martha cared about her household; Mary cared about what Jesus had to say. What do you care about? yourself? family? friends? Some of us don't care about anyone *but* our family and friends.

Some of us care only about our pleasures. Nothing comes between us and them; our fun comes first.

We care about money. We work hard and do almost anything to earn more money. We care about stocks and bonds, insurance and jewelry, property and automobiles, food and clothing, education and health. Those things we regard as valuable we never exchange for anything.

When physical disasters strike, we manifest a concern for the world: the San Francisco fire, the California earthquake, the Pakistani floods. We are generous to all manner of charities.

Yes, we care about many things, but do we care about the most important things? spiritual things? How many of us put God first?

Hundreds of thousands show no concern for the church. Many who do not are members who simply say, "I am not interested." A measure of love for the church is the tithe, for "where your treasure is, there will your heart be also." Plenty of members spend more on clothes, cars, homes, entertainment, tobacco, than they give to God. Do they really care?

Does anybody care about lost souls? Are valuable, priceless souls important to anyone? Does it matter to you that many souls are lost, without hope? that if they reject Christ their souls will be condemned to eternity in hell? condemned to a present hell?

The first question we should ask our preachers is, Do you love lost souls? Do you care? Not many professing Christians seem to care. If they do, they aren't showing it.

I am so grateful that somebody was interested in my soul.

Somebody wanted me to be a Christian, to go to church, to pray. If you have a godly mother, wife, husband, brother, sister, pastor, or friend, you are most fortunate. I will never forget the Sunday school teacher who took me home to dinner. If somebody hadn't cared for my soul, I wonder where I would be. If someone hadn't cared for you, loved you, trained you, spoken to you, shown interest in you, where would you be?

People appreciate nothing more than an interest in their spiritual welfare. A few may resent it—Jesus told us to expect mistreatment from some—but for every one who resents your concern, 999 appreciate it. During my entire ministry, my concern for them has been resented by only a few people.

It is sad when a church loses its passion for souls. One man told his pastor that he had attended church for three years without anyone ever asking him to become a Christian. When a church loses its passion for souls, it might as well close its doors, because it is going to die anyway. Churches that swell with pride, wealth, refinement, and culture until they need nothing and are unconcerned for the lost are the most pitiable.

One of the mysteries of human nature is the great interest parents can take in everything but their children's souls. How many people have said to me, "As far back as I can remember, I cannot recall my mother or father saying a word to me about becoming a Christian." And this from the children of professing Christians! Why? Why?

Doesn't our silence show how shallow is our religion? Should we not influence people? Do people know where we stand, or do we betray Jesus with a guilty silence? If I ask someone else whether you are a Christian, what will he say? Are you a Christian at home and not at work? Are you a Christian in the store, on the farm, in the office, at the lodge, at the country club, on your business trips, on the golf course?

Suppose a friend said to you: "I worked with and for you, waited on you when you were sick, discussed war, business, politics, books, and philosphy of life, but I can't recall your ever having invited me to become a Christian. I knew you were a Christian, and we were companions, friends, and associates, but you evidently did not care about my soul. I might have been saved if you had cared. I might have considered religion important if I had thought you did." How would you feel?

One mother told me that she had prayed for her son for forty years. He still was lost and she was about to stop praying. But I encouraged her to keep on, because her prayers might be answered while she was in heaven! She wasn't guilty of failing to tell her son; he had simply refused to hear the good news. She had tried to win him. We have no evidence that Jesus was able to win all of His family. Nor was He able to save the rich young ruler. God doesn't force people against their wills. He only requires that we do our best to win others.

If we are to care about the lost, we must realize what it means to be lost. It means going to the grave having rejected Christ. "As the tree falls so shall it lie." Jesus said to those who ridiculed Him, "Ye . . . shall die in your sins," and, "Whither I go, ye cannot come."

Death comes suddenly and unexpectedly, but we know it will come. Death is certain; what is uncertain is life! We should shudder when we consider the destiny of impenitent souls. We should be rushing to say, "While I have my wits, while my mind is clear, while the need is urgent and the danger imminent and apparent, I will decide the biggest question of all, calmly and gloriously, by surrendering to Christ."

"Jesus Careth for You"

Do you care about your own soul? Even if there were no heaven, would you want to live this life without Jesus? If nobody else cares for your soul, do you care?

One thing is certain; the world does not care about your soul. Clouds may burst, storms may come, torment may assail, but the world will not care about your soul; the world might give you money, fame, success; merchants might want your trade, politicians your vote, libertines your virtue, liquor dealers your business: but few will be interested in your soul. The devil certainly does not love your soul, and the world is his territory. He will lead you to indulge and, when you try to stop, will tighten his grip on you until you cry aloud, "Who shall deliver me?"

Lord Byron was an uncaring spirit of the world. At thirty-seven he cried, "Fill it again, the golden goblet, for I have drunk it dry. My days are gone; the world, the canker and the grief are mine alone." Edgar Allan Poe was a master of poetry but died unhappy and miserable. He saw the beautiful Annabelle Lee starve to death on a bed of straw in Richmond. He lost every friend. He wandered in Philadelphia, New York, and Baltimore and became a beggar, soiled, tattered, and disreputable. He died in a hospital, uttering, "Lord, help my poor soul." Irvin S. Cobb, comedian and man of many fine qualities, went to his grave not "soothed and sustained by an unfaltering trust," but with a cackle of forced and scornful laughter. These men had fame, but they had no peace, no happiness, no spiritual contentment.

Does all this mean that *nobody* cares?

No. Some do care. Some Christians care. Every brick, board, pew, and hymnbook in your church is evidence of that. Many whose hearts are burdened are giving their best, making every possible sacrifice. And these are going to keep on caring.

And Jesus cares, too. If He hadn't cared, would He have gone to the cross? He left His throne and the song of the angels to come into the world because He cares. Though our sins be as scarlet, though we are weak, frail, unworthy, sinful, tempted, and temptable, He cares. The world doesn't care; the devil doesn't care; a lot of people do not care: but Jesus cares.

If He cares so much, shouldn't we care just a little?

The Revival We Need / 11

Psalm 119:25

. . . quicken thou me according to thy word.

What is revival?

According to Webster's to *revive* is "to return to consciousness or life; to reinvigorate, rejuvenate, recover from a state of neglect or disuse, raise from languor, depression, or discouragement."

A religious revival is all of this in a spiritual sense: a quickening of the soul by God's Holy Spirit. The psalmist wrote, "Quicken thou me according to thy word."

A great man may preach a sermon with grace, wit, talent, and interest that you will never forget, but that's a revival not from the Holy Spirit but of the visiting minister.

A genuine revival results in an increase of spiritual life that follows scriptural guidelines. Revivals do not just happen. They are the result not of chance or luck but of much preparation.

True Revival

The kind of revival we need will, first, *bring a great conviction of sin*.

To be revived is to see sin as God sees it. Then we will want to do something about our troubled consciences, our worried minds, our aching hearts, our restless nights. We will ask, "What must I do to be saved?"

When David saw sin as God does, he said: "For mine iniquities are gone over mine head: as an heavy burden they are too heavy for me." And in Psalm 51:3: "For I acknowledge my transgressions: and my sin is ever before me."

God demands a humble and contrite heart; revival is impossible without it. "Godly sorrow worketh repentance."

We need to be told that we suffer from sinfulness, but we need more than a diagnosis; we need a cure. We need to tremble over our sins, to realize that we cannot save ourselves.

The kind of revival we need, if it brings conviction of sin, also will *bring conversion of lost souls.* These wandering sheep will be "pricked in the heart."

Third, the conversion of sinners will *restore the joy of salvation* to the many who were already converted but who have lost this joy. They were once happy and active in the church, but they have become estranged. They too, need to be convicted of sin, turned from it and revived. Then will their joy be restored.

Conviction, conversion, and joy will also *regenerate unregenerated church members.*

We need a revival first within the church. The greatest revival possible would result if unregenerate members laid their lives upon the altar of God. Sometimes it is harder to win the unsaved who are church members than the unsaved who are not. We need a revival that will touch the hearts of all men.

We need a revival that will *make workers out of shirkers.* We need to break the "do-nothing" bonds of the membership and make drones into busy workers. The church has too many IWW's ("I Won't Work"), too many flabby Christians whom the wind can blow about. We need undying loyalty, people who can be depended upon.

We need a revival that will *increase enthusiasm in church life,* an enthusiasm that will abide. One of the greatest needs in our churches today—and one that is being met outside the church—is the filling of the Spirit. The Christian church was born out of the great enthusiasm at Pentecost.

We need a revival that will *burden the hearts of Christians for the lost.* Some Christians have never won anyone. If there are any today who, like David, can say, "No man cared for my soul," then Christians are not doing their job. "He that winneth souls is wise." Their blood is on our hands; we are responsible for the wicked. If we shun, despise, hate, or discourage them, we do not have the spirit of Christ.

We need a revival that will *sanctify home life*. The institution of the family has suffered from divorce, separation, and children leaving home earlier and earlier, but that institution remains the foundation of the American republic. What a difference there would be in family life today if every family met regularly to share experiences with each other and with God.

We need a revival that will *increase and deepen our sense of responsibility and loyalty to the church*. We could use more John Knoxes. Our religion is too much like a ball of wax; it takes the shape of whatever comes into contact with it.

We need a revival that will *send us back to our Bibles*. Psalm 119 is a meditation on the law of God.

"Thy word have I hid in mine heart, that I might not sin against thee."

"I have rejoiced in the way of thy testimonies, as much as in all riches."

"I will delight myself in thy statutes."

"Open thou mine eyes, that I may behold wondrous things out of thy law."

We need a revival that will *rekindle brotherly love*. When we ask forgiveness of someone we have wronged or hurt and offer to shake hands, what a revival that will be.

"Love thy neighbour as thyself."

"By this shall all men know that ye are my disciples."

"Let love be without dissimulation."

"The Lord make you to increase and abound in love one toward another, and toward all men."

We need a revival that will *encourage stewardship*. Regeneration is the salvation of the soul; enlistment is the conservation of life; stewardship is the utilization of power and possessions. God wants souls that are regenerated, dedicated, and generous. The whole man given over to Christ is the only true evangelist.

We need a revival that will *increase church attendance*. Such a revival would bless all denominations. It would not be a narrow, bigoted, selfish revival, but one that would warm the hearts of all and send them, reconsecrated, back to the churches.

We need a revival that will *clean up whole cities* for Christ. A revival would affect our everyday dealings. It would produce honest merchants, godly doctors, truthful lawyers, faithful preachers, loyal citizens, devoted mothers, obedient children, industrious workmen, and Christian teachers.

We need a revival that will *have permanent, abiding effects,* a revival that lasts and is not "gone with the wind." We need a revival, not like the beautiful Siberian sunflower which pushes through the snow only to face the withering blast of evening and perish within a few hours, but a flower of faith and joy which, after blossoming, would live forever in the hearts of men, a flower like the rose of Sharon or the lily of the valley.

But How?

The question is, How are we going to have such a revival?

The psalmist prayed, "Quicken thou me according to thy word." This was a personal prayer. He didn't pray, "Quicken others," but, "Quicken me." If you are quickened, others will be. When you are on fire, you will discover combustible material all about you. All quickening is individual. At Pentecost "tongues like as of fire . . . sat upon each of them."

We must be born in prayer. At Pentecost they prayed for ten days. "Such as this cometh about only by prayer."

Pray for yourself until new life is infused, then pray for others. You do not need money, jewelry, fine clothes, education, honor, or position to have the ear of God. The person who feels least significant will be quickened first by the power of God. If you cannot pray, "Quicken thou me," pray for grace to pray, for the spirit of prayer, and for power. "Every good gift and every perfect gift is from above, and cometh down from the Father of lights."

Keep your eyes open, and tongues as of flame, purifying and enlightening, will appear on many heads and glorify them with the image of God. Keep your ears open, and the wind of the Spirit of God will blow through this old world now as always. When you see and hear it, say with Peter, "This is that which was spoken by the prophet Joel; . . . I will pour out of my Spirit upon all flesh."

Faith for Life's Storms / 12

Job 13:15

Though he slay me, yet will I trust in him. . . .

The Book of Job is a great drama of doubt. It depicts a battle between faith and the hard facts of life. We might call it the drama of the human heart or the epic of the inner life.

Perhaps this wonderful dramatic poem has no historical basis. It may, like Proverbs and Ecclesiastes, belong to the "wisdom literature" of the Bible. But to us the story of Job is real. His problems are ours. Our experience is similar to his.

The opening scene portrays a lovely picture indeed. "There was a man in the land of Uz, whose name was Job; and that man was perfect and upright, and one that feared God, and eschewed evil" (1:1). He was the richest man in the East, the father of ten children, seven of them sons. He feared God and hated evil, and he sanctified his home. "Thus did Job continually" (1:5).

In the second scene we witness a trial in heaven, something which Job and his friends did not see.

> Now there was a day when the sons of God came to present themselves before the Lord, and Satan came also among them. And the Lord said unto Satan, Whence comest thou? Then Satan answered the Lord, and said, From going to and fro in the earth, and from walking up and down in it. And the Lord said unto Satan, Hast thou considered my servant Job, that there is none like him in the earth, a

> perfect and an upright man, one that feareth God, and escheweth evil? Then Satan answered the Lord, and said, Doth Job fear God for nought? Hast not thou made an hedge about him, and about his house, and about all that he hath on every side? thou hast blessed the work of his hands, and his substance is increased in the land. But put forth thine hand now, and touch all that he hath, and he will curse thee to thy face. [1:6-11]

Satan was saying that man can trust God, but God cannot trust man. Try him, punish him, torture him, and man will quickly turn his back on God. But the Lord said, "All that he [Job] hath is in thy power; only upon himself put not forth thine hand" (1:12).

The third scene brings us to the trial on earth, Job's trial. God's man is put to the severest tests.

Loss of Property

First Job lost his property. When he was sitting in the city at the public gate in friendly conversation with those who esteemed him, one of his servants came running, saying that his cattle had been captured and all his servants slain. Imagine the shock and horror of passing, in one day, from riches to poverty! Poverty is terrible enough for one who has known nothing else, but for one who has been rich . . .

Suppose this should happen to you today. Suppose you should lose everything you possess. What difference would it make to you? The trial of one's pocketbook is often the test of one's faith. Job passed this test, saying, "Though he slay me, yet will I trust in him."

Loss of Loved Ones

Job's second trial was more excruciating than the first: he lost his loved ones.

For a father like Job, the loss of one son is a deadly blow. But the loss of all ten children, all at one time, would be virtually unbearable. Did ever a loving father suffer greater bereavement? Looking at the bodies of his ten dead children, he exclaimed, "The Lord gave, and the Lord hath taken away; blessed be the name of the Lord" (1:21).

What would you and I have done? There is a lesson here for us. I call all those who suffer to the feet of Job to learn, for he looked beyond his losses to God and clung to Him. He reminds us of Jesus of Nazareth who, in the Garden of Gethsemane, prayed, "Nevertheless not as I will, but as thou wilt." If we would drive away Satan and have the angels of God minister to us, we must have such faith.

Loss of Health

After Job had successfully stood the fiery trials of impoverishment and bereavement, Satan took away his health. Satan touched Job with the finger of disease and he contracted one of the most painful forms of leprosy: ugly, loathesome sores from the sole of his feet to the crown of his head. Poor, childless, diseased, Job went and sat among the ashes.

A tortured body is the acid test of faith. When the head throbs, the nerves lie exposed, and the body is racked with pain; when weariness and disgust fasten upon you because of dragging, failing health: that's when the will goes lame and moral failure takes over.

Robert Louis Stevenson made a great contribution to literature and left a splendid heritage of romance, but his greatest contribution was his buoyant hope and unconquerable good cheer while fighting the inroads of disease. Most of his books were written from bed, where his throat and lungs were torn by incessant coughing and his head reeled from sheer weakness. Facing death he wrote:

> Under the wide and starry sky,
> Dig the grave and let me lie,
> Glad did I live, and gladly die,
> And I lay me down with a will.

Despondency drove Moses out of Egypt, humbled Elijah under the juniper tree, made David play the fool before the Philistines, sent Judas to a suicide's grave; Job cried out, instead, "The Lord gave, and the Lord hath taken away; blessed be the name of the Lord."

Loss of Friends

After all this, Job lost even the confidence and esteem of his bosom friends. Three men were dear to him. When they heard of his misfortune, they visited him. His desperate condition so overwhelmed Job's friends that they rent their clothes and said nothing for seven days and nights.

After a while they became suspicious. Believing that adversity comes from wrongdoing, they said among themselves: "Good men prosper; bad men suffer. He was not so good a man as we supposed. He must have been secretly violating the terms of the covenant."

Imagine how hard this was on Job. No longer were these men friends; they had become enemies. Instead of comfort they brought condemnation. They misunderstood him and falsely accused him. He must have felt as David: "For it was not an enemy that reproached me; then I could have borne it . . . But it was thou, a man mine equal, my guide, and mine acquaintance. We took sweet counsel together, and we walked unto the house of God in company." Job was penniless, childless, healthless, and friendless, but he nevertheless lifted his voice to heaven and said, "Though he slay me, yet will I trust in him."

Loss of Helpmeet

What did Job have left?

His wife, his beloved. Her life had been spared. Sympathy from her would offset some of these trials and give Job a measure of comfort, but instead of sympathizing with her husband, she upbraided him with a cruel taunt: "Dost thou still retain thine integrity? curse God, and die" (2:9). The sorely tried man replied, "Thou speakest as one of the foolish women speaketh. What? shall we receive good at the hand of God, and shall we not receive evil? In all this did not Job sin with his lips" (2:10).

Job's faith did not shrink. He clung to the faithfulness of God. He had absolute confidence in God, for He was real to Job. He loved God, as the first commandment teaches us to, with heart, mind, and soul. He loved God better than wealth, family, health, friends, wife, or anything else. He knew that God would right all wrongs. Satan could not destroy his confidence in God.

We cannot always see the shore, but if we cling to God, He will bring us safely through. A severe storm once besieged a vessel at sea. A strong sailor chose a child to swim to shore with him. He said, "Put your arms tightly around my neck, and no matter what happens, don't let go." They plunged into the raging sea and the little fellow clung to the rescuer until at last they were safe on shore. If we cling to God, we will reach the shore.

A painter took a friend to his home to see one of his recent paintings. He conducted him first to a very dark room and left him there alone for a few minutes. When he returned, he explained that the guest would not have been able to appreciate the painting if he rushed into the studio with the glare of the street still in his eyes. The painter wanted to prepare him to perceive the painting's real beauty.

God wills that we wander into many dark rooms in order to perceive the glories that await us. We will be able to appreciate them more after having been in the dark.

> O for a faith that will not shrink
> Though pressed by many a foe,
> That will not tremble on the brink
> Of poverty and woe;
>
> That will not murmur nor complain
> Beneath the chast'ning rod,
> But in the hour of grief or pain
> Can lean upon its God;
>
> A faith that shines more bright and clear
> When tempests rage without,
> That, when in danger, knows no fear,
> In darkness feels no doubt.
>
> Lord, give me such a faith as this,
> And then, whate'er may come,
> I taste e'en now the hallowed bliss
> Of an eternal home.

A Call to Consecration / 13

I Chronicles 29:5

. . . And who then is willing to consecrate his service this day unto the Lord?

Someone asked Henry Drummond, "Isn't the first need of Christianity today that it shall have more men behind it?" He replied, "No, not more men, but a better brand."

Unless we are consecrated, our efforts are in vain. We can do without everything else, but we cannot do without that. Consecration is the supreme need of all Christians.

Numbers are important, but they are not *most* important. We need not just more men but more men who are on fire for Christ.

Money is also important, but it is not the chief requirement for the advancement of Christ's cause. We could use much more, but with all our wealth we could still be a dead, cold, lifeless church. However, if we are consecrated, we will give. Those who are the most generous givers are those who are consecrated.

Effective organization and cooperation are important, but unless the workers are consecrated, to what end are they working? If every superintendent, teacher, and student were consecrated to God, what a difference that would make. Would we not go forward?

If God's kingdom is to be established, we must go forward. But we will go forward only if we give ourselves. If we fail to give ourselves, we have not given all. The Bible everywhere magnifies the gift of self, of life, as the first requirement for advancing in the cause of Christ. No life can count for the highest or best unless it is yielded to Jesus.

Men of Consecration

Illustrations of the truth that the supreme requirement of Christians is consecration abound in the Bible.

Look at Amaziah, who "willingly offered himself to the Lord." Amaziah was Jehoshaphat's chief army officer, commander of two hundred thousand soldiers. This eminent leader put God's cause first. He gave God first place in a secular calling, a difficult place to serve.

Some say that doing what they do, they can't be consecrated. But a great pork packer in the Northwest, when asked what his business was, replied, "I am a Christian, sir. That is my business."

"You didn't understand. What is your daily work?"

"My business, sir, is to be a Christian, but I pack pork to pay expenses."

The greatest contribution any man can make is himself. To give himself willingly, without coaxing, urging, or persuasion, further enhances the contribution.

The great Gladstone once said, "Napoleon had the keenest brain that was ever packed into a human skull." But he died like a dog in a ditch after he had made Europe tremble before him. What did the sacrifice of one hundred thousand soldiers mean to his self-centered and fiendish ambition?

Selfishness always loses in the end, while

> He always wins who sides with God,
> To him no cause is lost.

One of the worst kings in the Old Testament was Ahaz, whose son was Hezekiah, one of the best kings. He opened the Temple doors which his father had long since shut. He attended to the religious needs of his people first, saying in effect: "Righteousness exalteth a nation: but sin is a reproach to any people." He called them to repentance. "Your iniquities have separated between you and your God, and your sins have hid his face from you, that he will not hear." He called for an offering and confessed his sins. "When the burnt offering began, the song of the Lord began also." A burnt offering symbolizes the dedication of one's life. When people dedicate their lives to God, His work goes forward.

David was another consecrated man. He encouraged Solomon to build the temple and gave him the plans. And when the gold, brass, stones and precious jewels, and silver were all collected, he asked the people to dedicate themselves willingly: "Who then is willing to consecrate his service this day unto the Lord? . . . Then the people rejoiced . . . because with perfect heart they offered [themselves] willingly to the Lord."

Caleb and Joshua must have been consecrated also, for God said that, of all those men twenty years or older who came up out of Egypt, only two would see the land which God promised to Abraham, Isaac, and Jacob: Caleb and Joshua. Only they had "wholly followed the Lord." Could it be said of us that we have followed Him wholly, or is His anger kindled against us?

In his Letter to the Romans, Paul pled for consecration: "I beseech you therefore, brethren, by the mercies of God, that ye present your bodies a living sacrifice" (12:1). And in II Corinthians 8:5, he tells us that the people of Corinth "first gave their own selves to the Lord, and unto us by the will of God."

Jesus pled for consecration in the greatest sermon ever preached: "But seek ye first the kingdom of God, and his righteousness; and all these things shall be added unto you." Seek God first—not second, not partially, not accidentally, but *first*—and the best shall be yours.

Consecrated to What?

Queen Esther was more concerned about saving her people than glorifying herself. There is great power in a consecrated life. The question is, Will we be consecrated to good or evil?

The story of Samson is one of the saddest in the Old Testament. Before his birth he was dedicated to God, and the Spirit of the Lord moved him. He was a strong man who judged Israel faithfully for thirty years, and the secret of his strength was his consecration to God, symbolized by his hair. When Delilah shaved his locks, his strength left because his consecration had left already. Without God, Samson was like other men. He lost strength, and he lost favor with God.

The ancient Romans were consecrated to battle: "I will conquer or die: the name of Rome is written on my heart. For my country to live or die; or to shed my blood." The Romans were consecrated to their country. To this day, let a man find a purpose and become absorbed by it, and what will he do? Die for it. Why not for God?

Dedication to God can be as real as dedication to country. Those who have been set apart, hallowed, devoted to God have endured unheard-of agonies: they have been sawn asunder, they have languished in prisons, they have been killed by the sword. They have defied tyrants, threatened, and dared. And what has made them heroes? Consecration to Jesus Christ.

Dwight L. Moody, whose lack of education and eloquence made others laugh at him for attempting to preach, won a half million souls to Christ because he was wholly consecrated to Christ.

Frances Havergal said, "There must be full surrender before there can be blessedness." After she had utterly yielded herself to Christ, she wrote:

> Take my life and let it be
> Consecrated, Lord, to Thee.
> Take my feet and let them be
> Swift and beautiful for Thee.
> Take my voice and let me sing
> Always, only, for my King.
>
> Take my hands and let them move
> At the impulse of Thy love.
> Take my silver and my gold.
> Not a mite would I withhold.
> Take my moments and my days.
> Let them flow in ceaseless praise.

Consecrated to God

Madame Guyon, whose prayers shook France, was torn from

loved ones, despised, persecuted, imprisoned, and exiled. She wrote:

> I have heard the voice of Jesus,
> Tell me not of aught beside;
> I have seen the face of Jesus,
> All my soul is satisfied.

Is your life consecrated to Christ?

Jesus does not limit your happiness, He increases it: "Thou wilt shew me the path of life: in thy presence is fulness of joy; and at thy right hand there are pleasures for evermore." He does not limit your power: "Then shall the righteous shine forth as the sun in the kingdom of their Father." He does not remove your freedom, He adds to it richness, fullness, grace, beauty, and an eternal noon of fadeless splendor. The Master is come; He calleth!

He came in stillness at Sinai and called Moses, and Moses became the greatest character before Christ. He came in the hush of midnight and called Samuel, and Samuel became the finest judge in Israel. He came in a lonely hour to Isaiah, and Isaiah became the greatest prophet. He came to Saul on the road to Damascus, and Saul became the greatest exponent of Christianity. He came to Peter and John at the Sea of Galilee and said, "Follow me, and I will make you fishers of men," and they became the two greatest disciples.

He comes to us today and calls us to rededicate our lives to Him and to His service. We can answer, as did Alexander Maclaren: "If you want to live in this world, doing the duty of life, knowing the blessings of it, doing your work heartily, and yet absorbed by it, remember that the one power whereby you can so act is, that all shall be consecrated to Christ, and done for his sake."

Gideon routed the host of Midian with three hundred dedicated men. John Wesley said that one hundred men consecrated to God could turn the world upside down. Moody said, "The world has yet to see what God can do with a thoroughly consecrated man." If all of us dedicate ourselves to the Lord, we can change the church and the world!

The Church in a Critical World / 14

Psalm 87:3

Glorious things are spoken of thee, O city of God. . . .

What is the purpose of the church in today's world?

Some tell us that the church no longer has any purpose and that it will pass away entirely in a few years. Some feel that the church should be a good-natured and kindly institution which tolerates things as they are and hopes only for mild change that is compatible with their vested interests. Some tell us that the church should do more to promote law and order and safeguard property values. Some say that it is valuable only to the faint of heart—timid women and effeminate men, the sad and the dying. Many complain that, whatever its purpose, it is not accomplishing it.

One thing is clear: the world is not satisfied with the church, yet the church stands. Everywhere we look we see churches. On every hand a spire points like a mighty finger to the sky. If the church no longer serves a purpose, why does it continue to last? Why are churches being built every week? If the church were a dead horse, would so many people be kicking it?

Whoever fears that the church has no place in our world does not understand the nature of the church. He certainly does not know the Lord and Author of the church, who "loved the church, and gave himself for it." He does not know the history of the church or its foundations, nor does he have the slightest idea what Jesus meant when He said, "Upon this rock I will build my church; and the gates of hell shall not prevail against it."

With all her imperfections, the church is still the most powerful force for good in the world. As such, her place in the world is secure.

A Reminder of Eternity

The church gives people today an eternal perspective. Man is born with a sense of the eternal. The Greek word for man, *anthropos*, means "upward-looking creature." Man is ever looking upward, away from ugliness to beauty, away from imperfect knowledge to the truth that sets us free. In the comradeship of the church we confess the age-long yearning of our hearts for God.

Some years ago a little church building on the coast of England was destroyed by a hurricane. The people were unable to rebuild it and had to worship elsewhere. Then a representative of the British admiralty came to the minister and asked if the building would be rebuilt. After the minister explained the insurmountable obstacles, the admiral replied: "If you do not rebuild it, we will. That spire is on all our charts and maps. It is the landmark by which the ships of the seven seas steer their courses." The church is a landmark for each of us; from the depth of its foundation to the tip of its steeple, everything in it points upward to God—to the eternal by which we chart our course on life's sea.

The function of the church today is to say, "You can bet your life there is a God."

A Defender of Human Rights

The church has always given untiring support to humanitarian enterprises.

Our first educational institutions were founded by the church. Today, the church operates hundreds of universities and colleges.

Our hospitals originated with the Christian ministry of healing. "Jesus went about all Galilee . . . healing all manner of sickness and all manner of disease among the people." The church of Christ has carried on this compassionate service throughout the world.

Where did present-day charity programs come from? The church has always looked with compassion upon those in need.

What about the great foreign mission enterprise? In his early years, Wendell Wilkie doubted the value of missions. A world tour he took shortly before his death changed his mind:

> I saw at first hand a multitude of concrete instances which convinced me of the value of foreign missions both to the lands they serve and to the cause of good will for America. Everywhere I went I found colleges, schools, hospitals, and churches, many of them supported by the churches of this land. I found American missionaries, men and women, exerting a leadership—a human personal leadership—which I have no hesitancy in characterizing as vital to the future hopes, not alone of other nations, but of our own United States.

The concept of liberty itself—the freedom to speak, think, write, and behave as conscience dictates—was born in the church. As Cardinal Newman said, "Not a man talks bravely against the church but owes it to the church that he can talk at all."

Albert Einstein spoke of the place of the church in today's world:

> Being a lover of freedom, when the revolution came in Germany I looked to the universities to defend it, knowing that they had always boasted of their devotion to the cause of truth; but no—the universities were immediately silenced. Then I looked to the great editors of the newspapers, whose flaming editorials in days gone by had proclaimed their love of freedom; but they, like the universities, were silenced in a few short weeks. Then I looked to the individual writers, who as literary guides of Germany had written much and often concerning the place of freedom in modern life; but they, too, were mute. *Only the church* stood squarely across the path of Hitler's campaign for suppressing the truth.

The church today not only defends human freedom sternly but also demands justice for the individual. Freedom is impossible without justice. The only essential equality is equality before God. The ground is indeed level at the foot of the cross.

A Uniter of Nations

One word describes the present world situation: *split*. The world is split into nations, nations into races, races into classes, classes into homes, and even homes into husband and wife, parent and child. The whole world is split. Something is missing. The church must accept its full share of responsibility for progressively ordering the world according to the will of God. Politics can't do it; money can't do it; physical force can't do it; only Christ and His church can overcome these divisions.

Whatever the future holds for the church, the church has learned in the last decade that it cannot be the church of Jesus Christ, who dwelt among men, and be isolated from the world. It cannot be content with lovely dreams, cherished ideals. It cannot be the church of the cross without declaring the gospel of redemption and witnessing to the power of His all-sufficient love. It cannot be a church that prays, "Thy will be done," and has no concern for the destiny of human lives.

The church is on solid ground when it prays and works for the unity of nations: "God . . . hath made of one blood all nations of men for to dwell on all the face of the earth." It is on solid ground when it educates people to honor every man for his worth and hate no man for his race or color: "God is no respecter of persons." It is on solid ground when it joins the hands of all God's children to make this one world for Christ: "Go ye therefore, and teach." It is on solid ground when it protests prejudice and ill will: "On earth, peace, good will toward men." It is on solid ground when it preaches the brotherhood of man: "If a man say, I love God, and hateth his brother, he is a liar." It is on solid ground when all its members say, "I go to church because I love the world; for there I hear a law that men should love one another with a love that stoops to the cross."

An Exalter of Christ

The church has survived for nineteen centuries with an unchanged message: at the center of all things is a living, dynamic force—Jesus Christ. The church's purpose in today's world is to point men to the redeeming grace of God as revealed in Christ on the cross. The business of the church is to exalt Christ: "The church's one foundation is Jesus Christ her Lord."

I know of no other force that changes lives as does Jesus Christ. Christ came to seek and to save. This is the mission of His church. No person is so sinful that he cannot be saved. Only the cross of Christ can reduce selfishness in the world.

The sacrifice of Christ, by which the world is reconciled to God, is the church's profoundest message. In the final analysis, it is the church's only message, for only the church proclaims it.

Glorious things of thee are spoken,
Zion, city of our God;
He whose word cannot be broken,
Formed thee for His own abode:
On the Rock of Ages founded,
What can shake thy sure repose?
With salvation's wall surrounded,
Thou may'st smile at all thy foes.

What's Your Excuse for Living? / 15

Genesis 5:27

. . . all the days of Methuselah were nine hundred sixty and nine years: and he died.

Every now and then someone commits suicide and leaves a note saying, "Life is not worth living." Somehow he is unable to adjust to life's problems and, in a fit of depression, takes his life.

Is life worth living? Solon the philosopher said, "Count no man happy until he is dead." And Clarence Darrow, a noted atheist, a few years ago advised young people to chuck it all and jump out of the window.

The problem of "realizing life" is not an easy one. A questionnaire listed sixty-five reasons why people are religious, and the reason most often checked was, "Religion helps me find meaning in life."

Sooner or later every person faces the question, "What is the reason for living?" "Do I have an excuse for being alive?" "Why should I be here?" "What am I doing here?" One man said: "The trouble with me is I have no reason for living. I see other people who seem to exist without any reason. They simply desire to obtain work to earn money to buy things to have a good time. An aimless existence is fit for an animal, but a man needs a reason and I have none."

Methuselah lived to be 969. Did he have an excuse for living?

Look at the records. He is mentioned seven times. Six times he is merely cited in some genealogical table. The seventh passage, our text, says in effect: "He lived thus number of years and died." His life may have been more interesting than these passages imply, but one wonders. Plenty of people live that way, only not that long.

On the other hand, one of the shortest lives recorded in the Bible lasted only thirty-three years. That life made an immeasurable impression. None could have estimated its power and influence on the past, the present, and the future. We marvel at the unparalleled splendor of Jesus' achievements, the sublimity of His example, the unwavering loyalty of His service. Looking at the record, we say, "What a life!" We see the value of Jesus' life not in its extent but in its intent and content.

Without divine purpose, life is meaningless. Think of the possibilities locked up in every soul: powers of the heart, mind, and soul which are denied every other creature. Man has a great capacity for fellowship with God which can be developed: "And Jesus increased in wisdom and stature, and in favour with God and man" (Luke 2:52).

In a book entitled *Things Men Live By*, Dr. Richard C. Cabot gives four reasons for living, four things we can do to get the most out of life.

Working and Sharing

One reason for being here is the work that needs doing. Jesus came "not to be ministered unto, but to minister." Few men ever worked as He did. "I am among you as he that serveth." "I must work the works of him that sent me."

For many, work is drudgery. They work day in and day out and have no love for it, no sense of mission, no feeling of cooperation.

Einstein said that, without the joy of cooperating with kindred minds in the pursuit of the unattainable in science and art, his life would have been empty.

We are creative individuals equipped to engage in creative activity. We want to do something worthwhile, not waste our lives in the desert. We want to repay the great Creator for letting us be a part of the world. Life becomes meaningful when, in small ways or high places, we are linked with others to help that which is true become real. Life should become increasingly useful; for it to become less useful is tragic.

Florence Nightingale had everything she could possibly want at home. But only when she looked at the desperate state of the nursing profession in her day and asked, "What is wanted of me?" did she discover what the real Florence Nightingale should become.

We hear a great deal about the waste of human resources. We are tempted in the computerized age to let machines take over completely and to let our powers lie dormant.

Do you ask, "What is my life worth?" It is worth only what you share, not what you possess. Some of the greatest men in history lived without possessions. Statistics show that the majority of significant persons in our history have lived in modest homes on humble incomes. Great people are not necessarily business giants who manipulate human needs for profit, but people who have learned how to share, how to give themselves.

After the first worldwide radio network was hooked up, a fox terrier barked into the microphone, and the sound circled the globe. Some persons have access to the ears of the world and seem to do nothing but bark. That's sad, because the happiest people in the world are those who give of themselves.

We are here to cooperate in the great enterprise of making the world better. If we do not join that enterprise, we miss the mark and do not live at all!

Playing

We can play as well as work. God knew we would work better for six days if we took one day off. Those who take the time to play enrich their personalities and spirits and minds. We need to "get off the earth" occasionally—not to escape life, but to return to it with new enthusiasm.

One reason our country could prepare for two world wars almost overnight was its stress on athletics. As long as we continue to love football, baseball, fishing, hunting, tennis, and sailing as much as we do, we are not likely to minimize the importance of play.

Some find their pleasure in great books. Archbishop of Canterbury William Temple said that Plato, the writer of the Gospel of John, and Robert Browning were the three greatest intellectual friends he had found across the centuries.

Some find their pleasure in music. Scarcely anything is more uplifting and balancing than listening to great music. Edna St. Vincent Millay's poem "Concert" tells of a girl whose lover wanted to accompany her to a symphony. She asked to go alone so that nothing would interfere with her pleasure in it. She bade him adieu:

> Come now, be content.
> I shall come back again to you,
> I swear I will,
> And you will know me still.
> I shall be only a little taller
> Than when I went.

Loving

Men also live for love. Love tells us life is worthwhile. Love tells us we are of value.

If the love of a loved one is sweet, how much sweeter is that of God, who loved us for all time, even sending His Son to die for us? When we are tempted to ask, "What is man, that thou art mindful of him?" we come to the foot of the cross and find our answer.

If we were like rubbish for the trash heap, if we were like the grass of the field and the birds of the air, if there were nothing beyond the grave, would Christ have died for us? No! Man is of inestimable value; he was worth the blood of Christ.

"God is love; and he that dwelleth in love dwelleth in God, and God in him."

Love never fails, bearing all things, believing all things, hoping all things, enduring all things.

Love can help us to better the world about us. In all areas of life, love is needed and effective.

After F. Scott Fitzgerald died, among his papers was discovered a list of ideas for possible future stories. One was particularly striking: "A widely separated family inherits a house in which they have to live together."

This brings to mind quite a picture! It could also bring to mind our world—a widely separated family. This world is a badly dilapidated house in which we all have to live together. We either live or die in it together, and the only way to live together is to love. Strikes would cease if employers and employees could imagine each other's point of view. Jews, Protestants, and Roman Catholics could resolve their problems through redemptive love. Racial prejudice, hatred, and indifference could be eradicated once we made the church and the community a place of brotherhood through redemptive love. "Not where I breathe, but where I love, I live," wrote Robert Southworth in "Made for Love."

Worshiping

We are also on this earth to worship. Our work, our play, and our love are regulated and integrated by our worship. If life is to be worth living, man must get all the help he can. The greatest help of all comes from worship.

A clock is constructed to accurately measure time. If all the parts are properly oiled and tuned, it will achieve its purpose. So with the noblest work of God: man. He is no mere fortuitous concourse of atoms or assemblage of cells; he is human and finite, a child of the eternal.

In "The Soul of a Bishop" by H. G. Wells, the bishop has an interview with the angel. The angel tells him:

> "All religions are trying to tell something which they do not clearly know . . . something that eludes the human mind as the water escapes from the hand."
>
> "And the truth?" said the bishop. "You can tell me the truth."
>
> The angel thrust his hand through the bishop's hair, ruffled it affectionately, rested it for a moment, holding the bishop's cranium in his great palm. "But can this hold it? Not with this little box of brains! You could as soon make a meal of stars. You haven't things to do with it inside this."

God has revealed only what man can understand. Incarnation is the key to life's glorious meaning. The life God would have us lead is pictured in Jesus. We "beheld his glory, the glory as of the only begotten of the Father," and He was " full of grace and truth."

Jesus' self-sacrifice showed us the life which is life indeed. As the poet has written:

> We live in deeds, not years; in thoughts,
> not breaths;
> In feelings, not in figures on a dial.
> We should count time by heart-throbs.
> He most lives who
> Thinks most, feels the noblest, acts the best.

Christ gives us a picture we can all understand. He reveals life as God intended it to be. "Man is meant for joy, not sorrow; for peace, not anguish; for love, light, and home, not for estrangement and exile." If we would see life from the divine angle, we must look at Jesus.

What a glorious privilege to come face to face with Jesus in worship! Emerson once said that a straw held parallel to the Gulf Stream would allow the waters to flow through it. Worship is like that. It allows God's love and energy to flow through us, and humbles us in the face of God's majesty.

It also teaches us to determine how best we can ally work, play, and love. Man is made for work, yet men allow work to interfere with worship. Man is made for play, yet men allow play to interfere with worship. Man is made for love, yet love without worship is cut off from the source of all love. What! you haven't any star and you're going to sea? you're going into battle with no music? you're going on a trip without a book? What! you have no love and yet you talk of living? We are here to work, play, and love, but the quality of each depends on the quality of our worship. The way we balance these four privileges determines the richness of our lives. Thomas Carlyle was right: "The longer I live, and I now stand on the brink of Eternity, the more there comes back to me that sentence which I read as a child: What is the chief end of man? To serve God here and to enjoy Him forever."

Worship to the human being is as the song to the thru physical grace to the tiger, or speed to the race horse. It justi man's existence and lifts him to the highest plane. To neg worship is to accept a low rating as a man—to become a spirit mummy.

Are you expressing your entire personality?

What is your excuse for living?

You CAN Go Home Again / 16

Genesis 35:3

> *. . . let us arise, and go up to Bethel; and I will make there an altar unto God, who answered me in the day of my distress, and was with me in the way which I went.*

In *You Can't Go Home Again,* Thomas Wolfe wrote:

> You can't go home to your family, back home to your childhood, back home to romantic love, back home to a young man's dreams of glory and fame, back home to exile . . . back home to lyricism, back home to aestheticism . . . back home to the ivory tower, back home to places in the country . . . back home to the father you have lost and have been looking for, back home to someone who can help you, ease the burden for you, back home to the old forms and systems of things which once seemed everlasting but which are changing all the time—back home to the escapes of Time and Memory.

The Hebrew children spent forty fruitless, futile years trying to go back home to an alien land.

> And all the congregation lifted up their voice, and cried; and the people wept that night. And all the children of Israel murmured against Moses and against Aaron: and the whole congregation said unto them, Would God that we had died in the land of Egypt! or would God we had died in this wilderness! And wherefore hath the Lord brought us unto this land, to fall by the sword, that our wives and our children should be a prey? were it not better for us to return

> into Egypt? And they said one to another, Let us make a captain, and let us return into Egypt. [Num. 14:1-4]

Some people have never had a home. They do not know what home is. Some go through life without a home. Many return to the place they left in the morning not because they are loved or wanted there but because they have no place else to go. They fool themselves into thinking they have a home when they have only a house.

Home is where you belong, where those are whom you love and who love you, where you know who you are.

If anyone was ever happy at home, I was. I shall never forget that day at Union Station when my loved ones came to tell me good-bye. I boarded a train and wept as though my heart would break. Being away from my people was hard for me. But the years have flown by and the home in which my mother and father lived has been torn down; every so often I get a notice that the weeds must be cleared off the lot. Visits to the empty lot and the cemetery send me hurrying back to Atlanta; everything has changed so. I cannot go back to the home that once was.

Away from Home

Many of us have wandered far from home, our true home in Jesus Christ. We have separated ourselves from the heavenly Father, wanting like Adam and Eve to be lord ourselves. We are not content to let God be God. We want excitement. We want to see what the world is all about. We give up our souls in search of a perpetual amusement park. We even become ashamed of our spiritual parentage, since God is hardly "cool" or "with it."

We not only seek to play God, we also attempt to live without grace. There is no justification to life apart from grace. Our lives have meaning because we are God's children. He loves us because we are His, not because we have earned His love. We would never be able to earn enough to pay our spiritual debt, but God paid the cost on the cross.

We have journeyed into a far country. Our spiritual condition is reminiscent of the prodigal son's, who lived without grace, enslaved to an alien self. When we really live, we live by grace at every level of human experience. Grace is undeserved love. We have belittled our relationship to God through idolatrous worship. We have shattered our brotherhood through selfishness and hate. We have destroyed the significance of sex by abusing it. We are in the midst of a famine, feeding on husks in our desperate search for significance, hungering for meaning that is not satisfied.

I am reminded of the pilot who called back to his passengers: "I regret to announce that we are completely lost and have no idea where we are or in which direction we are going, but you will be happy to know that we are making good time."

We are enslaved to hard taskmasters: sex, popularity, education, economics, and on and on. We are like the man who was caught in a shipwreck with a belt of gold around his waist. He refused to undo the belt and he drowned. He did not have the gold; the gold had him.

You may recall Charles Lamb's whimsical remark that his children were to be brought up in their father's religion if they could discover what it was. Much of our religion is superficial—a label with no contents.

That great preacher Hugh Latimer, while preparing to preach at the Royal Court, heard a voice saying: "Be careful what you preach today, because you are going to preach before the King of England." Then he heard another voice say: "Be careful what you preach today, since you are going to preach before the King of kings." Instead of preaching the gods we make, we should be preaching the God who made us.

Have you ever started across the street and suddenly noticed a car coming toward you? You are startled for a minute, and your feet either won't move at all or move in different directions.

We are living in a confused world, and we want to go home. But we are being told that we can't go home again. What shall we do? Where shall we go?

Home to God

We can go home to God. We can prepare for our eternal home. The Bible tells us we are on our way home. It tells of the prodigal son, who first had to "come to himself." He woke up; he made up his mind. He decided he had to do something.

To come home to God, then, is to do as the prodigal son did —acknowledge our sins, our separation from the Father, our waste of our inheritance. We need to admit that we have missed the mark, that we exist in the midst of a famine of meaninglessness, that we are enslaved, that we suffer from the indignity of gracelessness. The first step on the road home is to humbly admit that we have a long way to go. "I will arise and go."

Second, we must be willing to let God be God and to serve Him humbly. The prodigal decided to return home and say not, "Father, your son is here," but, "I . . . am no more worthy to be called thy son: make me as one of thy hired servants." When we say this sincerely, God welcomes us not as servants but as beloved children.

Third, those who once lived close to God but have drifted far away need to return to Bethel. Our text says on their behalf: "Let us arise, and go up to Bethel; and I will make there an altar unto God, who answered me in the day of my distress, and was with me in the way which I went."

Bethel was dear to Jacob. It was where God had revealed Himself to Jacob after he had deceived his father and stolen the birthright from Esau.

Isaac had sent Jacob to his Uncle Laban's in Haran to find a wife and escape Esau's wrath. Jacob stopped for the night, gathered stones for a pillow, and lay down to sleep. He dreamt of a staircase leading to heaven with angels hurrying up and down. Jacob became keenly aware that someone was leaning over him; it was God. Jacob said, "The Lord is in this place; and I knew it not. . . . this is none other but the house of God, and this is the gate of heaven." He renamed that ugly place "Bethel," meaning "House of God." And there he knelt and prayed as never before and consecrated his life to God.

Jacob left Bethel and moved on to Haran, where he worked for Laban. He worked hard, grew rich, and schemed. Living among wild and godless people, he forgot to erect an altar of public worship. And when you look at the sum of his life, you see failure.

How many leave Bethel and also leave behind their religion? That's when troubles begin. They become irregular at church and eventually give it up altogether. At first they feel guilty, then less and less guilty. They deteriorate spiritually and morally.

Jacob had no family altar for private devotion. Is it any wonder that things were going wrong? The first spiritual duty many people neglect is that of private devotion. How many people, if they were honest, could say: "The declension began in my inner life before it showed in my outer life. I deserted the altar of prayer and ceased to read my Bible?" They have no place left called Bethel.

Home to Bethel

In the midst of Jacob's sorrow and trouble, like a star shining through the clouds of a dark night, he remembered Bethel. He heard a voice saying, "Arise, go up to Bethel, and dwell there."

How could he go back to Bethel? Could he begin again? Could he make that back move?

Yes! He called his household to repentance, to put away the "strange gods" they had adopted, to cleanse themselves from idolatry, and to take the road back home to Bethel: "Let us arise, and go up to Bethel; and I will make there an altar unto God, who answered me in the day of my distress, and was with me in the way which I went."

God has a way of driving us back to Bethel to rededicate ourselves to him. Troubles are intended to teach us to remember. When God arouses our memory and memories assail our souls, we can go back.

Jesus went home again. In John we read that Jesus went back to the place where John had first baptized Him, where the dove of peace had settled on His head, where God had called Him to His life work, where He had dreamed big dreams. The wintry winds howled about Him, but He found rest, and He found His feet again. There He found strength for the dark hours that lay ahead.

God is calling you home today. You must go back to Bethel, the place of early dedication and consecration, and among those dreams of long ago you may dedicate yourself once more to God.

God is waiting for us at Bethel. We can take all our burdens on our pilgrimage, but when we get there we will share the burden. Then it will be loosed from our shoulders and rolled away into a sepulchre from which it will never rise again.

We can rebuild those first altars and call on the name of the God of Bethel. He will answer as He did in former days, saying, "Let the wicked forsake his way, and the unrighteous man his thoughts: and let him return unto the Lord, and he will have mercy upon him; and to our God, for he will abundantly pardon."

"When he came to himself, . . . he arose, and came to his father. But when he was yet a great way off, his father saw him, . . . and ran, and fell on his neck, and kissed him."

What a homecoming there will be when you go home again!

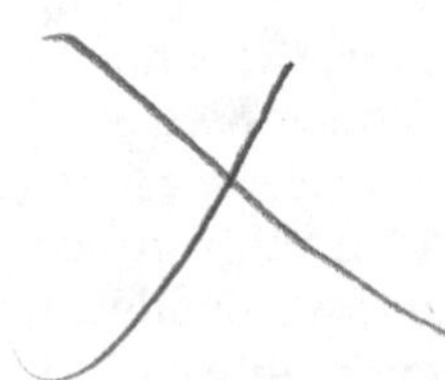

The Unfinished Task / 17

Hebrews 12:1

Wherefore seeing we also are compassed about with so great a cloud of witnesses, let us lay aside every weight, and the sin which doth so easily beset us, and let us run with patience the race that is set before us.

Some eighteen hundred years ago an unknown Jewish convert to Christianity wrote what is now known as the Bible's "Hall of Fame." In it he recorded the names of the great heroes of his race, men who in both war and peace had striven valiantly for the common good: Abel, Enoch, Noah, Abraham, Isaac, Jacob, Sarah, Joseph, Moses, Rahab, Gideon, David, Samuel—men "who through faith subdued kingdoms, wrought righteousness, obtained promises, stopped the mouths of lions, quenched the violence of fire, . . . turned to flight the armies of the aliens. . . . And these all, having obtained a good report through faith, received not the promise: God having provided some better thing for us, that they without us should not be made perfect" (Heb. 11:33-40).

A little over one hundred years ago a great American stood on the battlefield of Gettysburg and, thinking of the thousands who had died there, said: "It is for us, the living, to be dedicated here to the unfinished work which they who fought here have thus far so nobly advanced. . . . that we here highly resolve that these dead shall not have died in vain; that this nation under God shall have a new birth of freedom; and that government of the people, by the people, and for the people, shall not perish from the earth."

These two great speeches, one by an unknown Jewish convert and the other by President Abraham Lincoln, are separated by eighteen stormy centuries and are worded differently, but in meaning are very similar. Men across the centuries have lived and died heroically, yet the causes for which they lived and died have not always triumphed fully. Apart from us, such causes cannot triumph: "God having provided some better thing for us, that they without us should not be made perfect." Our lives are linked with the lives of those who have gone before us.

The author of Hebrews saw what wonderful faith his forebears had had, and how they had died with the promise of something better to come. We have the image; they had only the shadow of heavenly things. The inheritance that former ages sighed for has come to us. We have the manifested Savior, the outpoured Spirit, the full revelation. They had only the promise. Now they and we are to enter into perfection together. The boundary line separating us has been obliterated. Whatever blessedness belonged to those who died "in the Lord" belonged equally to their Old Testament predecessors. All the privileges accorded New Testament believers are theirs.

"Wherefore seeing we also are compassed about with so great a cloud of witnesses . . ."

Heroes for the Cause of Christ

Lincoln saw that the living were spared to finish the work of those who nobly gave their lives. He was thinking of our nation, but I am thinking of the church. How many have died for that cause! How many have given their best, their all. They have not given their lives in vain that our church under God might have a new birth. Christ's way of life shall never perish from the earth. The torch has been passed!

However, we need to remind ourselves that progress, while necessary, is not inevitable. It is not an accident. Light may become darkness. Gains may be lost. Advance may be followed by retreat.

As people live in the shadow of great universities who cannot read or write, so people live under the eaves of our churches who are lost. The dead are dead! They can only inspire us. What they lived or died to accomplish, we the living may advance or retard, conserve or destroy. Civilization is a cooperative enterprise involving the living, the noble dead, and the unborn. The dead can do nothing apart from us. If we leave unfinished the tasks which they so nobly began, those tasks can never be finished and their hopes will never be realized.

What are some of these unfinished tasks?

The Missionary Enterprise

The missionary enterprise has passed through several stages. The first missionaries sought to rescue people from hell in the hereafter, believing that the future for those who die without Christ is hopeless. Later missionaries became concerned with rescuing people from hell in the here and now, believing that men who live without Christ have no hope in the present. Then missionaries moved from the assumption that the West was Christian and the East pagan to a realization that paganism is found among all peoples. "What about the paganism at your doorstep?" is the first question the modern missionary may encounter. These missionaries believe that the West no less than the East needs to be brought under the influence of Christ—that unless people of every nation can be induced to accept Christ and exhibit more of His spirit, the world situation is hopeless. They realize that it is Christ or chaos for all the world.

What characterizes all three phases of the missionary endeavor is a common concern for the highest welfare of other people. Not the doctrines, the schools, the hospitals, or the churches, but the concern for human beings and souls is the distinctive contribution of the missionary venture. Missions has called the world's attention to the Savior, and to the notion that God cares, loves, lives, gives, and redeems!

Will we keep alive this long-range concern for the ultimate welfare of other people or will we let it die? It can be easily lost. The missionary enterprise can be junked if greedy commercialism spreads unchecked to the far corners of the earth. Apart from us, missions will fail.

The Fight for Freedom

What about the fight for freedom? Freedom is essential to the welfare and progress of the human race. Leo Tolstoy once wrote a letter to a friend complaining of Russian censorship. He spoke of the effect it had on his own mental activity. He wanted to write what he felt, but when he sat down to do so, he found himself considering what he would be permitted to publish or forbidden to publish, and he found it impossible to write anything.

Suppose William Tyndale had not claimed and exercised a freedom he did not possess? After betrayal by a friend, he was speedily imprisoned for translating the New and Old Testaments into English. He was cast into prison, kept there for a year, then strangled and burned at the stake.

What if over three hundred years ago a small group of Christians being persecuted in Europe had not brought wives and children across three thousand miles of sea to a new continent to face the odds, establish a foothold in the wilderness, and worship God according to the dictates of their consciences?

As the missionary enterprise is never finished, the fight for freedom is never won. Won by one generation, it must be won again by succeeding generations. It cannot be passed from one generation to another; each must win it for itself.

All of our freedoms were bought with the blood of our fathers. Each is guaranteed in the Constitution, yet each has been denied through the years. Apart from us, the valiant dead who gave themselves for freedom would see the fulfillment of their hopes to the end of time.

The Battle for Peace

So it is with the battle for peace. Tom Kettle of the University of Dublin expressed the hope that he might live to see the end of a war that was destroying his city and the beginning of understanding and reconciliation. With all of his hatred of war, he took up arms to help win a victory that would give peace to mankind. In the trenches he wrote that he had

> Died not for flag, nor king, nor emperor,
> But for a dream, born in a herdsman's shed,
> And for the secret scriptures of the poor.

War settles nothing; it unsettles everything. It is selfish and stupid and benefits nobody. A British cartoon said, "If war is hell, why not send it where it belongs?" War will go where it belongs only if we *send* it; it will never go of its own volition.

The Preservation of the Faith

Let us consider what has been happening to the church. People throughout the land have been turning away from organized religion as we know it and toward Eastern mysticism, drugs, and emotional and secularized Christianity. We cannot take this trend lightly. We are faced with a national dilemma which our forefathers may never have anticipated.

Marvin J. Taylor writes: "Perhaps the greatest contribution that the Supreme Court has made is to force upon us this much needed reassessment of the kind of religious training which is mandatory for achieving the quality of Christian nurture which the society of our day desperately requires." The court has ruled that public schools can teach *about* religion but they cannot teach religion itself. What will the church do about this? How will it respond? Our only recourse is to fall back upon the home and the church. Each generation must make its own educational programs work. Christian education is no more a finished task than are the missionary and evangelistic tasks. We must not beat a retreat. We must witness to Christ in ways that meet the needs of people—in ways that express the greatest concern for the welfare of men's souls.

A steam engine pops off steam only when it stands still or goes downhill. Let us stop popping off steam, change gears, and get to the task.

We must agonize. Have you had pangs about your church recently? Have you suffered on its behalf? Have you spent time on bended knee, examining your own life, asking where you are and where you are going spiritually? We will never fulfill the work begun by those in the "great cloud of witnesses" unless we agonize.

We must mobilize. We aren't going to win the world to Christ by letting our ministers do it alone. Every man and woman must be committed to the task. We must get ready for action!

We must visualize. We must look up and get a fresh new vision of God. We need to comprehend God's power and compassion. We need to see through the eyes of Jesus.

We must evangelize. We stand on the threshold of a brand new era, the "greening of America." Hope, optimism, realism, and honesty are being reborn in our youth and in our adults. The field is ripe for harvest; only reapers are needed.

Only the living can carry the torch. "From the honored dead we take increased devotion to that cause for which they gave the last full measure of devotion." We may resolve that these shall not have died in vain, that our church under God may have a new birth, and that the work of Jesus Christ shall never perish from this earth.

Among those who died for us, the chief is Jesus Christ Himself, who "loved the church, and gave himself for it, . . . That he might present it to himself holy and without blemish." He cannot do this without our help, but through us God can bring it to pass.

The unfinished task is ours to finish. The torch has been passed!